CONQUERING THE FILM AND TELEVISION AUDITION

Kevin Scott Allen

ReAnimus Press

Breathing Life into Great Books

ReAnimus Press
1100 Johnson Road #16-143
Golden, CO 80402
www.ReAnimus.com

ISBN-13: 978-1522887454

First ReAnimus Press print edition: January, 2016

10 9 8 7 6 5 4 3 2 1

Contents

I would like to dedicate this book to my students. Watching their successes, no matter how big or small, is what inspired me to write it in the first place. I thank them for allowing me to help them fulfill their dreams.

And I urge everyone everywhere to not just let their dreams lie dormant, but to pursue them.

For a dream not pursued is like a true love never kissed.

ACKNOWLEDGEMENTS

I want to thank Cherie Franklin, an amazing actress and the first teacher who really made a difference in my life. What I learned from her fuels me each day. Among the many things she taught me is that a script is so much more than merely words an actor speaks.

I want to thank Alan Feinstein, another amazing actor and teacher. I found Alan after working as an actor for years, so many years that acting had become just a job for me. I thank Alan for bringing me to a place where it became, once again, not just a job but a joy. His guidance has not only helped me to become a much better actor, but a much better teacher as well.

Then there is my manager, Anita Haeggstrom. Her counsel, friendship and care have been invaluable to me through these many years. Thank you so much for making this journey with me. Without you I'd still be wondering where to find the stage door let alone how to open it.

And last but not least, Bill Santoro. His thoroughness in helping me examine every word, his insistence that I not only write my ideas and thoughts but that they be written in the best, most easily understandable manner possible is what led to the creation of this book. Without him it would not exist.

PREFACE

Audition, audition, audition. It's a mantra that won't stop and the thing that is on most actors' minds, constantly. For the professional and budding actor alike, obsessing over the audition process can take over your whole mind and body, rendering you a helpless blob tossed around by the evil audition gods like a ribbon in a hurricane.

"What do I do to get one? How do I stop judging how I'm doing when I'm in the *middle* of one? What do *they want*? How do I *know* what they want? How do I *be* what they want?"

These thoughts sear your brain, never letting you go, taking all the joy and fun out of acting, turning it into a torture that must be endured if you're to survive.

Well, maybe I'm going out on a limb here, but I suspect that none of you reading this book chose to become actors to willingly immerse yourself in unending painful and debilitating torture. If by chance any of you did, I suggest you put this book down right now and carry on, letting your auditions terrify and imprison you in a world of constant agony. For those of you who seek to turn this evil monster into a friend and *take charge* of your Film and Television auditions, read on. This book will demystify the Film and Television Audition.

BUT CAN'T THEY SEE HOW BRILLIANT I AM?

Every day, of every month, of every year someone arrives in Los Angeles, New York, Chicago, London, or any number of other countless cities with one goal in mind: becoming a Film or Television Actor. Some have no experience whatsoever, others have degrees from prestigious universities, and others still have a list of stage credits five pages long. Some have acted on Broadway, others only in their living rooms. But they have come for the same reason and that is to act on screen.

Unfortunately, no matter what their background, most are woefully unprepared. Because no matter how big your talent or how extensive your experience and training, there is one major obstacle that stands in the way of your dream: the Film or Television Audition.

"I'm not worried," some of you might say, "I was the best in my class, the most talented, I've been in 30 shows, and I've won awards!"

All that may be true, but it won't be enough. Especially in a film capital such as Los Angeles. Let me use a buddy's story to explain.

A good friend of mine was telling me about his first day at college, Harvard. He felt great. He was going to *Harvard*. He deserved it. He had worked incredibly hard all through high school, got terrific grades, took on extra classes, had very high test scores, and was Valedictorian at his graduation. He had always felt special; until now. Because as he looked around him, as he talked to fellow freshmen, he realized they *all* were *just as special*. All of them had gotten terrific grades, had very high test scores, and most if not all were Valedictorians of their own classes. At Harvard, he was just another student.

So no matter how incredibly talented you undoubtedly are, no matter what credits you have, just look around you anywhere you go. Chances are there are people right next to you who are just as talented, with just as many credits as you. But you are all in the same situation. No matter how talented or credited you are, none of those things will be enough to launch your Film or Television acting career.

You have to know how to get a job. And to get a job, you have to Audition. But you have to more than just audition. You have to do more than give a *good* audition.

If you want to succeed, you have to know how to give a **great** audition.

This book breaks down all the necessary elements needed in a great Film or Television Audition. It explores every aspect of the Film or Television Audition, from your first preparation to your final call back. It takes the terror out of the audition by giving you necessary tools to give an *authentic* and *exciting* audition, each and every time.

You'll learn how to prepare for a Film audition and how to bring into the audition room the confidence and knowledge of a seasoned professional.

You'll learn the difference between a Film Audition and a Television Audition.

You'll learn the differences between various types of Television shows and the specific requirements needed when auditioning for each type.

You'll learn what is essential when auditioning for a Series Regular, a Guest Star, a Co-Star, and a One or Two line role.

But best of all, you'll learn how to bring into the Film and Television room something no one else ever can: the uniqueness that is you.

By the end of this book you'll no longer care about *trying to be* what they want.

You will have learned how to *make them want what you are.*

INTRODUCTION

WHO ARE THESE PEOPLE AND WHAT DO THEY WANT?

Before we get to Who they are, understand one thing: NOBODY KNOWS WHAT THEY WANT. Seriously. *They* may have some ideas based on the script and character descriptions, but those are just exactly that; ideas. That's why they're holding auditions. They want to meet actors and see what the actors bring to the table. If they already knew what they wanted, they wouldn't spend the time and money holding auditions, they'd just offer the role to someone they already knew. The very fact that they're holding auditions tells you they don't know they want.

Let's start by debunking myth of They. Who is this mystical, ever-to-be-feared *they*, this ever present boogie man of all actors? Got news for you: *they* are not bad people. There is no "they" monster hiding under the bed, or in plain sight in the audition room just salivating at the prospect of you failing the audition miserably. What does exist is a collection of very real, very human people who sincerely want you to make their day better by casting you. So before we go further, let's meet these people.

Anyone in any aspect of this industry can be of any sex. I have worked with some terrific writers, producers, directors and casting directors of both sexes. But for the purposes of brevity I am going to use "he" consistently throughout this book when describing people in general.

The Writer. The person who created the material by putting pen to paper, or more likely, fingers to computer keys. Sure the writer created the characters and probably has a complete mental image of each character and his personality. But the very fact that this Writer chose to present this story via moving pictures rather than a book means that he at the very least is open to having his mental image fleshed out by a real, live person. That is why the Writer chose to tell his story via the screen, and this means the story will have to be put together via a production team.

The Producer. He read the writer's story and decided to spend the time and effort to make it into something audiences would watch on a screen. The Producer has his own vision of the characters, and no matter how meticulous the writer was in his specific character descriptions, there is no way the Producer's mental image of each character is the exactly same as the Writer's. In fact, often the Producer's image is vastly different from the Writer's.

The Director. He has been hired to put the story together. He has his own mental image of each character, perhaps similar to, but sill different from the Writer's and the Producer's images of these characters; sometimes the Director's images of the characters may be vastly different from the Writer's or the Producer's.

The Casting Director. Hired by the Producer to find actors who *generally* fit the Writer's, the Producer's and the Director's images of the characters. This is easier to do if the Writer's, Producer's and Director's images of the characters are similar. But even if they're similar, they are never exactly the same. So the Casting Director's job is to bring in enough of a varied group of actors so that the Writer's, Producer's and Director's ideas of the characters are all represented. But on top of that, a good Casting Director will also bring in actors who represent the Casting Director's own image of the characters, which could be different from the Writer's, Producer's and Director's images. Many Casting Directors are famous for bringing in one or two *Wild Cards*, actors who don't seem to fit *anyone's* stated image of any of the characters, but whose unique characteristics might serve to tell the story in a different but possibly much more interesting way.

And this is just the *bare bones* version of a production team. Depending on the medium you might have to add any number of Network Executives, Studio Executives, Distributors, Executive Producers, ad nauseam.

Now take all these people and not only their own, personal images of who the characters are but also their knowledge of who the other team members' images of the characters are. Add to that the probability that they all will all have to come together at some point and compromise, and you will see that, in truth, NOBODY KNOWS WHAT THEY TRULY WANT.

So, for all you actors who sabotage yourselves by picking up a script, or *sides* (which is what the material you're given for an audition is called) and immediately point out why you're completely wrong for a part, "I'm too young, too old, too blond, too dark, too nice, too edgy, too inexperienced, too *anything*," STOP RIGHT NOW. You were called in to the audition for a reason. No matter what you think the sides say about the character, someone, somewhere, saw something in you that might be perfect for the role.

So let's *get to work.*

CHAPTER 1

THE FILM AUDITION

Now that we've established that no one really knows what they *want* from auditioning actors, there are some things that they *need*. A script goes into production because it is a story the production team wants to tell. Saying that this team doesn't know what it *wants* means that the team hasn't locked down *how* they want to tell the story, at least in terms of the actors. Every actor who walks through the door offers the potential to tell the story in his or her unique way. But there is still a story that must be told, and to tell any story there are certain things that are needed. To find them let's examine the film story a bit.

A film is open-ended time wise, meaning that though there are suggested lengths for each genre, there are no hard and fast rules regarding time. The generally accepted average length for a picture is between 90 and 120 minutes and in any film each scene can be merely seconds or minutes long. A film can tell its story without the specific and steadfast limits of a television program. In television, as we'll cover in the next section, each genre has very specific rules regarding timing, which means the story has to be told differently than how it would be told in a film.

That's not to say there aren't rules governing the structure of stories in film. There are most certainly specific story elements that are necessary, such as the Introduction, Set-up, First Act Break, etc.

I would recommend every actor read at least one book on screen-writing regarding film structure to better understand the way a film story is told (See "Recommended Reading" at the end of this book). But these elements in film story-telling are much more flexible than in a television story.

Because of this and because the writer of a feature film story has to fill at least 90 minutes, the story in a film is told through the main characters' *journeys*. Therefore it is essential when audition-ing for a film that the actor recognize and embody the journey of the character in whatever scene they're given to read. And though the journey of any character as presented in the film as a whole may be quite large, within any given scene the journey is usually fairly *small; subtle* but *specific*. As an actor it is your job to recognize each scene's journey, no matter how small and/or seemingly in-significant. Only by recognizing each scene's journey can you give an audition that will show the team you have the ability to tell their story and that you recognize the skeleton of the story. For that's what the character journeys are; the skeletons of a story. You, the actor, provide the flesh on the skeleton.

That's not to say that any story can only be told one way. Sto-ries may be told in any number of ways, through any number of different journeys. It's up to the actor to see the journey that is most likely present based on everything in the sides. We'll break down sides later to discover ways to do this.

Right now, let me give an example of what I mean by the char-acter's journey. Let's take a very popular main stream picture the 2012 film *The Amazing Spiderman*. The *story* was told via the *journey* of Peter Parker, the character who would become Spiderman. By breaking the story down into just a few sections, you'll see what I mean.

In the beginning, Peter is introduced to the audience as a nor-mal boy whose life takes a horrible turn for the worse when his parents disappear. He is taken in by his aunt and uncle who raise him as their son.

Fast forward to present-day before Peter is bitten by the spider. Peter is a photographer nerd. A beautiful classmate asks him if he is free after school. Peter thinks it's for a date, but she wants him to take photos of her boyfriend. In another scene he steps in when the class bully is beating up another boy. Peter is no match for the bully and gets beaten up for his trouble. But he is saved by the beautiful classmate, Kristen. A number of things happen in this scene but Peter's personal journey is internal and small.

Let's examine and break down this scene to find Peter's personal journey. What happens in the scene?

"Peter distracts a bully from beating up a helpless and weak classmate in front of a group of fellow students. Peter is attacked and beaten up until another classmate, Kristen, stops the attack by distracting the bully." Simple description of the *action* in the scene.

Now, let's view the scene from inside Peter's head and heart.

"Peter, seeing a fellow student being beaten by the school bully, makes a decision to try to stop the beating. Peter knows he's no match for the bully but his moral compass won't allow him to ignore someone in need. Peter, despite feeling his own fear of the bully, stops the bully from beating up a classmate. Peter's fear is realized when the bully attacks him. Peter is relieved when Kristen steps in to stop the bully. He is embarrassed he had to be saved but glad he was saved. He wonders if Kristen saved him because she might possibly like him or just because he was weak and needed saving."

There's a little more going on when we add Peter's *feelings* to the description of the action. But we can break this down to a much simpler definition of Peter's journey. Let's look at the above description of the scene again. By focusing on the *verbs*, it's easier to see the journey.

"Peter, *seeing* another weaker boy being beaten by the school bully, *makes a decision* to try to stop the beating. Peter *knows* he's no match for the bully, but his *moral compass won't allow* him *to ignore* someone in need. Despite *feeling his own fear* of the bully, Peter *stops* the bully from beating up a classmate. Peter's *fear is realized* when the bully *attacks* him. Peter *is saved* when Kristen steps in to stop the bully. He is *embarrassed* he had to be saved but *relieved* he was saved. He *wonders* if Kristen saved him because she might possibly like him or just because he was weak and needed saving."

So, whittling it down even further:

"Peter *sees* injustice, *is aware* of his own weakness but *decides* to step in, *fears* he'll be hurt badly, is *embarrassed* but *relieved* when he is saved, and *wonders* if Kristen likes him or thinks he's weak."

Whittling even further:

"Peter *decides* to allow himself to be physically hurt by the bully and at the end *wonders* if he should allow himself to be emotionally hurt by Kristen."

This leads us to Peter's specific journey in the scene:

Peter travels from willfully accepting physical vulnerability to being wary of emotional vulnerability.

All these scenes mentioned are in the beginning of the film when the story is being set-up, but journeys take place in every scene throughout this and any other movie. Even in the middle when he first meets Kristen's father, the chief of police, his journey is fairly small though this is probably the scene with the biggest journey for Peter. He goes from secretly sneaking into Kristen's room to having dinner with her family where he vigorously defends Spiderman against Kristen's father's accusation that Spiderman is a vigilante and common criminal.

If you haven't seen this film for a while, watch it again. Or watch any film. Pay attention to each scene, noting where the characters are in the beginning of the scene and where they are at the end. The journeys aren't *always* small; sometimes they are quite expansive, such as a scene where an unsuspecting husband comes home only to be completely broadsided by his wife telling him she's leaving him and their son, as in the beginning of *Kramer vs. Kramer*. But most scenes in most films contain small journeys. And even when a journey is large it is almost always large on the inside only. We'll discuss this further in the next chapter when we discuss playing the journey.

The film story is told via the main characters' small journeys for a reason. As I said earlier, films are anywhere from ninety minutes to more than three hours. A general rule of thumb is that one page equals one minute of screen time. So a 2 hour film would have a script of around 120 pages. An average scene in a film script is about 2 pages, so figure a 2 hour movie would have about 60 scenes. That's 60 sections of the main journey. With so many sections, the journey in each scene has to be relatively small and subtle otherwise the journey would be over far too soon.

Knowing this is how film stories are constructed it is the actor's job to correctly identify the character's journey in each scene, or side. Properly identifying this journey and bringing it to life is what every film side, and therefore every film audition, needs. The production team needs to see that the actor understands the script, understands how film stories are told, understands the scene and understands the journey of the scene. If an actor doesn't understand all of these things in one or two sides, most likely the production team will not trust him to understand them in an entire film. Time is money and there is no time these days for anyone on the production team to hold the actor's hand and guide him through every moment of every scene.

EXERCISE

DISSECTING A FILM

Watch a film you've seen before. I say this because I don't want you to get too caught up in the story. If you can watch it with the ability to pause it, so much the better.

On a piece of paper, write down each scene after it ends. Write down what happens in the scene and see if you can identify every character's personal journey in the scene. What happens in general? What happens to each character? Which character or characters *push* the scene and which character or characters *react* to events set in motion? Once you have the action of the scene, whittle it down as much as you can until you can state every character's journey in one sentence.

Do this for as many scenes in the film you watch as you want. After some practice, it will be easier and easier to do.

CHAPTER 2

DISSECTING THE SIDES

It's one thing to be able to identify a journey in a scene you see in a film and another thing to do it for sides, especially if you're only given one or two scenes from the film and not the entire script. When you watch a film, the actors are, hopefully, emotionally full and the journey is easier to see. When you read sides, all you get is a bunch of words on paper.

But therein lies the secret: *WORDS*

Words are the tools writers use to tell their story. They are the pallet of colors of a painter, the notes of a musical piece, the composition and exposure of a photographer. But you must do more than just read the sides; you have to *dissect* them. When you do this carefully you will get all you need to know about any side you're given.

WHAT MAKES UP SIDES

As I mentioned previously, *Sides* is the term used to describe the material you're given for an audition. It is a piece of the script. Depending on how large a role you're auditioning for, it may be one scene and only one page to many scenes and many pages. But even if you're auditioning for a one line role all sides contain certain elements.

A film script, or screenplay, is made up of a series of scenes. These scenes contain Action paragraphs and Dialogue.

ACTION PARAGRAPH EXAMPLE:

```
INT. DINER - NIGHT

Melinda sits in a corner booth. The glar-
ing overhead florescent lights bounce off
the faded and cracked orange vinyl uphol-
stery and accent the grease stains on the
wall of the open kitchen. She looks up as
JARROD ATKINSON opens the front door of
the diner. He stands in the doorway as if
he's not sure he's in the right place. He
sees Melinda. She lifts her hand and
gives him a small wave. He smiles and
walks over to her booth.
```

This tells where we are and what the camera will photograph. It describes the location and physical movements.

In the Action Header the first abbreviated word, INT means interior, or inside. If it were an outside scene, the Action Header would be EXT., meaning exterior.

The second word, DINER, tells us it is inside a Diner.

The third word, NIGHT, tells us it is at night.

The rest of the paragraph goes on to describe the diner and the physical actions of Melinda and Jarrod.

Notice that "Melinda" is not capitalized. This means this is not the first time we've seen her character in the film.

The fact that JARROD is capitalized means it is the first time his character is seen or heard in the film.

Dialogue is anything that is spoken. Each time a character speaks, the character name will appear above the words spoken.

DIALOGUE EXAMPLE

                              MELINDA
                 Jarrod? I'm Melinda.

                              JARROD
                 Hi. It's nice to meet
                 you.

If the role you're auditioning for is in the entire scene, then you'll be given the whole scene. But even if you're not given the entire scene because you're reading for a role that only has one line, your sides will include any and all location and action information needed for you to understand where you are and what is happening before your line and what happens right after it.

Here are three, short sides. Read through them. We will be using these as we discuss how to dissect a side.

SIDE ONE

INT. DINER - NIGHT

Melinda sits in a corner booth. The glaring overhead florescent lights bounce off the faded and cracked orange vinyl upholstery and accent the grease stains on the wall of the open kitchen. She looks up as JARROD ATKINSON opens the front door of the diner. He stands in the doorway as if he's not sure he's in the right place. He sees Melinda. She lifts her hand and gives him a small wave. He smiles and walks over to her booth.

                    MELINDA
          Jarrod? I'm Melinda.

                    JARROD
          Hi. It's nice to meet
          you.

Jarrod stands at the edge of the booth,
not sure what to do.

                    MELINDA
          Why don't you sit
          down?

                    JARROD
          Oh, yes. I… thanks.

Jarrod sits.

                    MELINDA
          Did you have any trou-
          ble finding this
          place?

                    JARROD
          No, your directions
          were perfect. I've
          never been here be-
          fore. It's… it's
          bright.

                    MELINDA
          Yes it is, isn't it?
          Not too flattering.

                    JARROD
        I think you look you
        look great. Just like
        your picture.

                    MELINDA
        Thanks. So do you.
        Look like your pic-
        ture. And great, too!

They both laugh. Jarrod looks around for
the waitress.

                    JARROD
        You want to order
        something?

                    MELINDA
        Only if you let me pay
        for myself.

                    JARROD
        Wow.

                    MELINDA
        What?

                    JARROD
        Nothing. It's just
        nice to meet somebody...
        somebody like you.

They both smile at each other. Melinda
catches the waitress' eye and nods. The
waitress winks at her as she walks over
to the booth.

SIDE TWO

INT. LARRY AND JULIE'S BEDROOM - NIGHT

Julie is sitting at an antique dressing
table putting cream on her face. She
catches sight of her wedding ring in the
mirror. She freezes for a moment, staring
at the diamond as it reflects light onto
her face.

She looks up to see Larry quietly opening
the bedroom door. He stops when he sees
Julie's reflection in the mirror and
their eyes lock on each other for a moment. Julie looks away and Larry comes
in, closing the door.

                    LARRY
              Wasn't sure you'd
              still be up.

                    JULIE
              You didn't tell me not
              to wait up.

                    LARRY
              No. I didn't think I'd
              be home this late.

                    JULIE
              Meeting run long?

                    LARRY
              Yeah. I couldn't get
              away.

Larry throws his coat on a chair. He
walks over to his dresser and takes off
his cuff links.

                    JULIE
          Did you eat?

                    LARRY
          Yes, Dave ordered in
          some dinner.

Julie watches Larry in the mirror.

                    JULIE
          The hotel called. You
          left your credit card
          at the front desk.

Larry pauses a second before he puts his
cuff links on the dresser and turns to
look at Julie in the mirror.

                    LARRY
          I must have left it
          there at lunch.

                    JULIE
          They have it for you.
          Along with the ear-
          rings the maid found
          in the room.

Larry stares at Julie. She turns to face
him.

                    LARRY
          Julie…

>   JULIE
>   Who is it?

>   LARRY
>   You don't know her. I
>   didn't want you to
>   find out like this.

Julie throws her hair brush at Larry.

>   JULIE
>   There's a good way to
>   find out your hus-
>   band's cheating on
>   you? How's that done,
>   Larry? With flowers?
>   Candy?

>   LARRY
>   I don't know, how
>   about finding his
>   socks in the laundry?…

>   JULIE
>   You bastard! That was
>   ten years ago. And I
>   ended it.

>   LARRY
>   Oh, so that makes it
>   ok? Just like it never
>   happened.

>   JULIE
>   Are you going to end
>   it?

> LARRY
>
> I don't know.

> JULIE
>
> I want you out of
> here. Now.

Julie grips the dressing table to keep herself from shaking. Larry grabs his coat and walks out, slamming the bedroom door.

SIDE THREE

EXT. METRO CLUB ROOF DINING TERRACE - DAY

Clifton is sitting at a table looking out over the city. He looks at his watch.

> CLIFTON
>
> Where the Hell is she?

A WAITER walks by.

> CLIFTON (Cont'd)
>
> Waiter. Bring me a
> scotch rocks.

> WAITER
>
> Yes sir.

Eleanor walks up to the host's desk. The host looks up.

                              ELEANOR
                    I'm meeting Clifton
                    Harding.

                              HOST
                    Mr. Harding is at his
                    usual table.

Eleanor looks around the room. Every table is seated, but she is the only woman
present. She stands there, smiling as she
sees Clifton.

                              HOST
                    Shall I escort you
                    there?

                              ELEANOR
                    I can find it myself,
                    thank you.

She waits a few seconds then walks to
Clifton's table. Clifton sees her approaching, but doesn't get up.

                              CLIFTON
                    I thought we said one
                    o'clock.

                              ELEANOR
                    We did.

The waiter sets Clifton's scotch on the
table.

                    WAITER
          May I bring you some-
          thing to drink, Miss?

                    ELEANOR
          No thank you.

The waiter walks away. Clifton picks up
his menu.

                    CLIFTON
          I'd like to order
          soon, I've got to get
          back for a meeting
          with the auditors.

                    ELEANOR
          There's no rush.

                    CLIFTON
          I think I can dictate
          my own schedule, if
          it's all right with
          you.

                    ELEANOR
          Actually, it's not all
          right with me.

Clifton puts his menu down and stares at
Eleanor.

                    CLIFTON
          What did you just say?

ELEANOR
Did I not speak
clearly?

CLIFTON
Who in the Hell do you
think you are?

ELEANOR
I'm the new chairwoman
of the board of direc-
tors, that's who I
know I am.

CLIFTON
What?

ELEANOR
Go call your buddy Ad-
dison Banks. He
doesn't like it any
better, but there's
nothing he can do
about it either.

CLIFTON
I don't know what
you're up to, but you
won't get away with
it.

ELEANOR
Well, it seems I al-
ready have.

Clifton throws his napkin on the table
and stands up.

```
                CLIFTON
      I'll bury you.


                ELANOR
      Fine, but you'll have
      to do it from some-
      where else. Your of-
      fice has been packed
      up. Everything is
      waiting for you at se-
      curity.


Clifton storms off as Eleanor reaches
over, takes his glass of scotch and takes
a drink. She smiles as she looks over the
city.
```

Now that you've read the sides, let's begin. Take out three pieces of paper so you can write down your dissections of each side separately.

1st DISSECTION

DISSECTION PREPARATION, or PREP WORK

Where do you begin? Exactly…

WHERE is exactly where you begin.

Where does the scene take place?

Always begin your dissection with WHERE before you go any further. The location not only sets the stage, it affects everything and everybody in the entire scene. Two people talking in a restaurant are going to be affected by the environment of the restaurant far differently than they would be if they were having the same conversation in a hotel room bed or in an office. You're going to go through the dissection list several times, so the first time through, be general and brief.

Look at the first side.

```
INT. DINER - NIGHT.
```

Write on the first piece of paper WHERE: *In a diner*. Very brief and general, but perfect for the first time through. We'll get more involved later. Take the other two sides and do the same thing.

WHAT

What is happening in the side? Merely write down what occurs without adding a viewpoint, justifications, or excessive detail. Many actors feel that they have to write down every single thing that happens in the side, but it is not helpful. In fact, it is counter-productive in the first dissection. The more bogged down you get with writing every little thing that happens in the side, the easier it is to get lost in the details and completely miss the bigger picture of what is happening.

A very easy formula to remember when dissecting the bare facts of the *What* is to focus on ***Direction/Change of Direction***.

Let's take the second side. What is the first thing that happens?

Julie is sitting at her dressing table.

She is doing various things while at the dressing table, but all that she does is part of the same direction. The first thing that happens that introduces something *new* to the scene is when Larry enters.

DIRECTION: Julie is sitting at her dressing table
CHANGE OF DIRECTION: Larry enters.

Even though Larry entering doesn't cause anything big to happen, it changes the whole dynamic of the scene for both characters internally.

Julie and Larry converse, but nothing happens either in action or in dialogue to change the scene significantly until Julie mentions the earrings. At that point Larry's affair is exposed, and everything changes.

CHANGE OF DIRECTION: Julie mentions the earrings the hotel found and Larry admits to having an affair.

The next change doesn't occur for several lines.

CHANGE OF DIRECTION: Julie demands Larry leave.

So a simple *What* of the scene is:

> Julie is at her dressing table when Larry comes in the bedroom. They both are getting ready for bed when Julie tells Larry she knows he's having an affair and Larry admits to the affair. Julie demands Larry leave and he does.

Simple and to the point. For this first dissection this is all we want.

WHEN

When is it? Night? Day? During a party, in the middle of a funeral, the match point of a game?

WHO

List every character in the side. A Business Man, his Wife, their teenage Daughter and the Dog. Be general, without any qualifiers.

Don't write An Angry Man, His Cheating Wife, their Thieving, Disrespectful Daughter. The man might appear to be angry in the side, his wife may actually be cheating on him, and their daughter might be the biggest thief in the state, but at this stage just list a basic description of each character in the scene.

2nd DISSECTION

Now go back to the sides and add more specifics based on what is written in the sides. Don't just add details because they might be fun or because you think it would make the sides more interesting. Trust me; there are usually plenty of details already written. You just have to find them. But *Find* them, *don't make them up.*

To do this, use a set of magic tools: ADJECTIVES, ADVERBS and VERBS

The Adjectives, Adverbs and Verbs the Writer used give you incredible amounts of specific information. Do not gloss over them, but underline them.

WHERE

What does the side say about the location? If it takes place in a place that serves food, as do both Side One and Side Three, what kind of place is it? What does the side say about the place to give you a more descriptive picture than just "A Diner" or "A Restaurant?"

What *Adjectives and Adverbs* does the writer use to describe the location? Is it *busy*, only a few customers, *darkly* lit? Really try to paint as full a picture as you can, based on what is written in the sides. Look for any and every detail you can find, no matter how small it might be.

Don't only look at the scene description, look at the dialogue. Are there any clues in the dialogue as to what kind of place it is? In Side Three, after Eleanor sees Clifton, the Host's line, "Shall I escort you there?" tells us this is not just a restaurant but a very formal restaurant.

WHAT

What is happening in a more detailed manner? Start with the 1st Dissection *What* and pay close attention to your behavior and the behavior of any other character in the scene. What does the specific, described behavior tell you? Are there any physical actions described? What are the *Verbs* the writer uses? In Side Two does Julie *toss* her brush or does she *throw it*; does the side say Larry *walks out* or does it say he *slams* the bedroom door as he leaves? Verbs are a terrific clue as to the *tension* level in a scene.

Look at the dialogue as well. Does anyone say anything that clarifies the *What*, or is the *What* clarified more by what isn't said? In Side One's dialogue Jarrod and Melinda are very courteous with each other, which not only tells us theirs is a brand new relationship it also tells us a lot about who they are. In Side Three the dialogue makes it quite clear that Eleanor has taken charge despite what Clifton wants or says.

In Side Two, the fact that the earrings were found that afternoon presents a much different feeling to the scene than if they had been found months before and Julie just didn't say anything.

A good way to further specify your work during the 2nd Dissection is by choosing stronger verbs in the descriptions you write. In Side One is Jarrod just *talking* to Melinda or is he *flirting* her? Are they both just *being polite* or are they both a bit *nervous*? Does Larry merely *confirm* Julie's suspicions about his affair, or is he *confessing* it? How does Julie react? Does she *accept* what he says or does she *argue* and *demand* to know whether Larry plans to end the affair? The stronger the verb or verbs, the clearer the *What*. But make sure the strong verbs are coming from what is written in the sides.

Does anything that you've added to your 2nd Dissection *Where* affect the 2nd Dissection *What* in any way? What does it say about

Side One that Jarrod and Melinda are meeting in a cheap diner instead of an upscale coffee house? Does anything you've discovered in the more detailed *What* tell you more about the *Where?* Knowing Eleanor is meeting Clifton to fire him, how does the detailed information of the restaurant being a regular place for Clifton affect you?

WHEN

On what page do the sides begin? Chances are the sides have been copied directly from the script, so the page should be in the upper right corner. What is the number? Is it near the beginning of the script, below page 10, or is it near the end, somewhere from page 80 on? If it's near the beginning, it's part of the set-up of the whole film.

If it's night, how late? Midnight, early evening? In Side Two it is fairly late as Julie is getting for bed. How is the *Where* affected by the *When?* Night at a diner is a lot different than Night at a dance club. In Side Three it is lunchtime, so Clifton is being fired in the middle of his work day, which is different than being fired over dinner.

An important aspect of the 2nd Dissection of *When* is to look at it in terms of the each character's life. In Side One it is not only night but the first time Melinda and Jarrod have met. Jarrod's last line, "It's nice to meet somebody… somebody like you" strongly implies he's met a number of people who aren't like Melinda. So this is a new and welcome experience for him. In Side Two an important character *When* is ten years after Julie had an affair of her own. This is a *When* she insists should have been forgotten, but one obviously Larry hasn't. What are some character *Whens* for Side Three?

WHO

This time, focus on your character. *Who* are you in relation to the *Where*, the *What*, the *When* and to the other characters? Are you a man who is so eager to have a relationship he has agreed to meet a stranger at night in a cheap diner? Are you a woman, the new chairwoman of the board of directors of a major company, who is meeting the president of this company for lunch in order to fire him? Are you a man who is still bitter over his wife's past affair?

Look at your *Who* in relation to the expanded *Where*. If Larry is truly determined to make his wife pay for her past affair, his *Where*, the bedroom he and his wife shared, is a three dimensional reminder of his marriage and of what he will be giving up if he leaves. In Side Three Eleanor not only chose to fire Clifton in the middle of a work day, she chose to do it at Clifton's regular lunch restaurant, a place where he is used to having all the power. What does that tell you about Eleanor? About Clifton and how this action would affect him?

How does the expanded *What* affect your *Who*? In Side Three, Julie has known about the earrings for some time. What does it say about her that she didn't call Larry and confront him with the information on the phone, but that she waited for him to come late at night?

WHY

Now that we know more about the sides and the people in them, we can look at the *Why*. *Why* is this scene taking place? Do this from two perspectives.

> *Story* Why and *Character* Why

A simple formula for finding an accurate Why, is to add a *reason* to any scene's What.

CHARACTER WHY

Why does the scene in Side One happen from *Jarrod's* perspective? If the What is that he and Melinda meet for the first time, let's add a reason: *so he can find out if Melinda is someone he wants to date* is one. What would be a possible *Why* for Melinda? Is it the same? *Why* does the scene in Side Two take place from both Julie's and Larry's perspectives? Julie knew about the affair earlier in the day, why did she wait to confront Larry? Why did Larry not make up a lie to try to cover?

STORY WHY

The Story Why answers the question "*Why* is this scene necessary to further the story?" The Story Why has two parts: *Scene Why* and *Writer's Why*.

For the first part, the *Scene Why*, combine all the characters' Whys for an overall *reason*. For Side One, two people meet on a first date in a diner *so that they can get together*. For Side Two, Larry's confesses to his affair and when he refuses to end it Julie kicks him out *so that both their lives change drastically*. What are some of the reasons why the scene between Eleanor and Clifton happens?

The second part, the *Writer's Why*, has to do with what the *writer's reasons* are for creating the scene the way he did. With these three Sides we don't know any more about the stories than what these sides tell us, but if you use your imagination you can come up with a number of reasons *Why* the writer created the scenes the way he did.

In Side One, what are some of the reasons the writer would chose a cheap, well-lit diner? Is it to tell us both characters are very down-to-earth? Is it to start their relationship in a fairly bland, neutral place so it can soar later? Why did he choose a glaringly bright place instead of one not so well lit? In Side Two, why would Julie confront Larry in the bedroom and not the living room? In

Side Three why doesn't Clifton take out a cell phone and call his buddy Addison Banks at the table instead of storming off?

It doesn't matter that you don't have more of the story, think of reasons of your own as long as they don't negate the information you have been given.

THE JOURNEY

By combining your *character's* Why and the *story's* Why, you discover your journey for this side.

Let's take Jarrod in Side One. The story's *Why* is so that they can meet face to face, in a place so well lit they can't hide anything physically about themselves, and begin a relationship to lead us to the next scene, and eventually to the end of the picture. Jarrod's *Why* might be that he is ready to take the next step and actually meet the person he's been corresponding with on the internet. His journey: *mustering up the courage to enter the diner, meet his contact and decide to trust her enough to take the relationship further.*

For Side Two take Larry's *Why* of confessing to his wife and walking out because he refuses to end his affair and the Story *Why* of needing to have Larry leave so that his and Julie's lives will never be the same. His journey in this scene is *admitting to his wife he's having an affair, refusing to break it off thereby pushing his life down an uncertain path.*

In Side Three, if Eleanor's *Why* is to declare she's in charge and the Story's *Why* is to set up a major conflict between Clifton, or the established order, and Eleanor, what would her journey be?

3rd DISSECTION

Go through the sides one more time. This time, as you look at all the elements of the dissections write down how each element makes you, the character, *feel*. Don't try to decide how you *should* feel, or what would be most *dramatic* feeling; simply how you *do* feel. You've read the sides several times by now, you've got a good idea of who you are. You know where you are, when it is, why you're there and with whom you interacting, now let the words of the script all combine to stir up feelings.

Use short sentences to describe your feelings about each element, using the strongest words possible, both adjectives and verbs. For the 3rd DISSECTION start with WHAT.

WHAT

What happens in the scene from your character's point of view? Though the action of each scene is constant, how each character feels about what happens is vastly different. In Scene Three what happens from Eleanor's point of view is the opposite from what happens according to Clifton's point of view.

WHERE

As you look over the *Where*, how does it feel to be where you are, especially now that you've looked at the *What* from your character's personal point of view? For Jarrod in Side One, do you feel degraded walking into a cheap diner, or relieved because your prospective date won't expect you to spring for an expensive dinner? Does the excitement of meeting her for the first time overshadow the place? In Side Three, how do you, as Eleanor, feel as you stride into the Metro Club, an obvious Old Boy's Club? (Note I wrote *stride*, not walk, because that is how I felt after I reviewed all I've written about that piece.) In Side Three, how do you feel as Larry entering your bedroom knowing you were in a hotel bedroom just a few hours ago with another woman?

WHEN

If it's late at night, after everything that you've discovered in the sides, how do you feel? Does time even matter? How do you feel about the interaction you're about to have after everything that's happened so far? In Side Three, if you're Clifton, how does it make you feel that Eleanor is late? In Side One, how does the time affect either your feelings? Are you excited that it's night and it's possible that you might go home together?

WHY

How do you feel about the reason you're where you are, when you are and with whom you are? Combining what you've discovered about all the elements above for Jarrod, are you excited about meeting this online date, nervous, frightened, or disgusted that this the only way you can get someone to go out with you? As Larry how do you feel about confessing to your wife, in *your* bedroom, at *this* time, both time of day and after the affair has progressed to this level?

WHO

Take all the sentences you've written about your feelings regarding the elements so far and combine them into a sentence describing who you are.

SIDE ONE EXAMPLE- JARROD: "I am nervous about meeting this person for the first time, relieved it's in a neutral place excited to see if we can connect for real, hopeful we can connect, and if we do, ready to plunge ahead."

SIDE TWO EXAMPLE – LARRY: "I am walking out on everything I've known for an uncertain future." Or "I hate everything about this room and can't wait to attack my wife with the confession that I've been having an affair and am dumping her for someone who really loves me."

SIDE THREE EXAMPLE - ELEANOR: "I am Chairwoman of the Board of Directors and am confident as I stride into this restaurant, a typical 'old boy's club', knowing I am the most powerful person in the room."

After you've carefully dissected a side, you will have loads of information. Great. Now what? What do you do with it?

What you do with it is the subject of the next chapter: Choices.

Before we proceed to the next chapter, read the three sides in this chapter again. If you haven't already done so, go through them and dissect each one for both characters. If you did dissect them earlier, now that we've really gone into detail about the three dissections, how do your dissections hold up? Did you take in all the details and information in the script? Can you make your dissections more thorough, more unique to you? What personal buttons are pushed in these sides, both good and bad?

CHAPTER 3

CHOICES - THE ONES ONLY YOU CAN MAKE

Now that you've done your Prep Work dissections, read through the side again, SILENTLY. Read every word. Visualize in your mind what is happening in the side. See your journey in your mind.

How is the story told to *accent* your journey? Do the sides progress through the journey *visually* and through *physical actions*, or do they progress primarily through the *dialogue*?

In Side One there are physical actions to be sure, Jarrod *enters* the diner, he *walks* up to Melinda's table and he *sits* down. But the story and his journey really progress in *response* to the *dialogue*. Melinda invites him to sit down, their conversation puts them both at ease and Melinda's telling Jarrod she'll pay for herself makes him realize she is different from other girls he's met. So Jarrod's journey is pushed along via the dialogue throughout the entire scene. In Scene Two, though much of the story conflict is revealed through the dialogue, there are quite a lot of physical actions that move the journey. Julie's whole behavior in front of the mirror, Larry's quietly entering the bedroom, his throwing his jacket down, Julie's watching him in the mirror, all leading to Julie throwing her brush and Larry storming out.

Once you've dissected the sides and pinpointed your journey, it's time to put it all *inside* you. All the dissecting in the world won't do a bit of good if it remains simply words on paper. By putting your Prep Work inside you, allowing it to *affect* you, you are able to do more than just understand the side; you're able to *live* it.

How do you do that? You start by making some *choices*.

WHAT IS A CHOICE?

A *Choice* is the way *you* interpret a side and the way you *navigate* the journey. It is your singular viewpoint and *How* you express it. Every person is unique and different from every other person. Sometimes by a lot, sometimes quite subtly, but we all have our own way of viewing and reacting to the world around us. So, even if ten actors work on the same side and interpret it almost identically, the way each actor *expresses* that interpretation will be unique to each of them.

A serious word of caution here.

A choice is not something that can't or must not ever change.

It is merely an *initial* interpretation you are making based on the work you've done thus far. Remember, at this point you're making these choices in a "closed environment." You're relying solely on your reactions to what is happening in the side and your gut feeling as to how any and all other characters are reacting as well. Things could change drastically when you read the side with someone else, either a Casting Director or another actor. They will bring their own choices which may or may not be what you expected. But you have to start somewhere. And the best place to start is with your own, strong choices.

STRONG CHOICES

"Make strong choices." Casting Directors say that over and over to actors. "Your choices weren't strong enough." What do they mean by that?

A "choice" is a decision an actor makes about how he is going to interpret and express a portion of the side. Note I said "portion." Nothing in life is static. Only in an artificial world do things not change. Change is life, but in order for something to change we have to start somewhere. A "strong choice" is a viewpoint that is *clear* and *easily identifiable*.

Making a weak choice is the number one cause of an unsuccessful audition. And the opening choice is the trickiest one of all.

Let's take Side One from the last chapter, our internet date scenario.

Weak Choice: "I'm curious about meeting her."

You've spent a good amount of time online with this person, exchanging enough information about each other to decide to meet in person and the best you can come up with is "curious?" I'm curious about how a pickle-flavored potato chip will taste when I glance at the package in the grocery store. Yes it's an honest reaction but hardly a strong enough one to launch into an audition. For that is what the beginning of an audition is, a *launch*. You're setting yourself and the entire scene up.

Strong Choice: "I'm nervous and excited about meeting her, though I'm going to work like Hell to hide it." See how much more is there? How much more is going on before the interaction even starts?

Let's look at Eleanor in Side Three.

Weak Choice: "I'm meeting a businessman for lunch." This choice says nothing. It's as if the whole life of the character just began a second before the scene begins. It says nothing about who you are, why you're here nor what you expect will happen.

Strong Choice: "I'm going to approach Clifton like a lioness stalking a mortally wounded hyena." You come in revving your engine and anyone watching will be glued to you to see if you instantly devour the man or toy with him first.

Every side you read is a *continuation of life* that started long before the side began. There is history that has happened and if you
don't embody a sense of that history, you start flat and weak.

*A strong opening choice is one that possesses the character's history
and uses it as a springboard to propel an actor into a side full of life.*

MAKING THE FIRST CHOICE

Take any or all of the three practice sides and review the elements, the Where, When, Who and Why for one of the characters
in each scene. Review these elements as they pertain to the very
beginning, the first time we see your character.

What is the *first* thing you *do*? Is it an *action* or is it *dialogue*? If
it's an action, what kind? Do you enter the scene or are you already there and you *do* something, such as Julie in sitting in front
of a mirror putting cream on her face?

If you enter, why are you coming in? What made you, as the
character, decide to enter this place at this time in your life? How
does your entering affect the story? Do you have an idea how the
other characters might react to you entering or are you completely
unaware of how they might react? It seems clear that Eleanor
knows exactly how Clifton is going to react to her entrance, but
Jarrod probably has no idea how Melinda will react. What if she
doesn't like what she sees? What if she isn't even there?

If the first thing your character does is an action, whether entering the scene or a physical act, how can you describe it in a sentence, using the clearest possible *verbs* and *adverbs*? Does Jarrod
simply *enter* the diner or does he *walk in shyly*? Does Julie just put
cream on her face or does she *examine* herself, both visually and by
touching her face with her hand? In an audition you most probably won't actually *enter* or even *do* an action such as putting cream
on your face, but you need to have a clear mindset and attitude of
the first choice, the first thing your character does. The mindset of
this choice will show in your eyes and affect your whole demeanor. This is the first thing you do so it says to anyone watching

as well as the other characters in the scene *who* you are and *what is going on inside of* you at this moment. How you interpret this choice doesn't need to be *big*, just *clear*.

If the first thing you do is speak, then what is going on that makes you speak? Are you asking a question, such as Melinda saying "Jarrod?" or Clifton talking to himself, "Where the Hell is she?" How can you express why you say what you say in the clearest terms possible? What choice will make it crystal clear what you *feel* in this moment?

SUBSEQUENT CHOICES

Not all choices will be equally as strong. The way a scene is usually structured, the characters enter into it from someplace, either physical and/or emotional, something happens in it and they leave the scene from someplace else, most often emotional. Therefore the *strongest choices* need to be paired with the strongest *changes of direction*.

As you read through the side, note any time the side changes direction, either through action or dialogue. Each time it does, another choice is present. How did it change direction? Was it through an action, such as Eleanor walking up to Clifton's table, or was it through dialogue, such as Julie bringing up the earrings. How does this change in direction affect the dynamic between the characters? How does it change the direction of the story? Sometimes a change is obvious, such as a strong reaction to whatever caused the change in direction. When Eleanor declares that she is the new Chairwoman of the Board it is pretty clear that Clifton is going to have a strong reaction to that news. The change could be small, maybe brought on by one word such as when Jarrod says "Wow" after Melinda tells him she intends on paying for her own meal. With that one word he just took the dynamic from polite niceties to expressing something heartfelt. What does Jarrod's one word response do to you as Melinda? How does the abrupt change of the dynamic make you feel?

An *action* could also signal a change such as when Julie throws her brush at Larry. That action changes the scene from a discussion to physical violence. How does that change affect you?

As you go through your side, don't just settle for the first choice that comes into your head. Though many times the first choice is correct, it may not be *specific enough*. Really examine it. Is it uniquely specific to you and how you feel? We all see things differently, so even though ten actors may see a moment in a side as something that makes them angry, your choice of anger needs to be put in a way that speaks to *you* in *your unique way*. I like to add a sentence to each choice that explains what it means to me, that pushes the particular buttons I see being pushed in me.

Let's take the moment of Julie throwing her brush at Larry and Larry's reaction to it.

EXAMPLE: "You always blame me for everything! *You* and *your betrayal* ten years ago caused this. You're to blame, not me!"

If whatever is happening in a side produced a feeling of anger, by pinpointing what *triggered* that anger and making it *personal* affects me in a way just writing "anger" couldn't. My choice isn't just "mad" it's "mad and hurt because of years of betrayal." Also, the more specific you are in your choices, the easier it will be to make adjustments later. But we'll cover that in another chapter.

NOT ALL CHOICES ARE EQUAL

Always come in with a strong choice and leave with one. You've come from somewhere into this scene for a reason, even if it's just entering a restaurant to get something to eat. That doesn't mean you come in screaming for a menu, it means you come in with the purpose of getting something to eat, not because you happened to wander into a restaurant doorway and thought, "well the script says I come in so I guess I come in." As the side goes on, usually the first change of direction is fairly substantial. Look at it carefully. Most writers create a world and then throw something in to disrupt it. The scene proceeds on a new course with some minor changes until something else comes in and disrupts it further and sends it in another direction.

Not all changes are equal, some are serious changes of direction and some are merely adjustments. In the Diner side, Melinda asks Jarrod to sit down and he does. This is an important, but relatively small change of direction for Melinda. She made up her mind to get to know him when she saw him at the door. If she didn't like what she saw, she never would have waved him over. So this is more of an adjustment than a change of direction. She has adjusted the direction of their interaction by asking him to sit down.

A much stronger change of direction is when Eleanor tells Clifton she's the new Chairwoman of the Board. That presents a serious challenge to Clifton.

The serious changes need strong choices. That's not to say that the adjustments don't need clear choices as well, but they're not as strong in that they don't create a whole new direction or change in attitude, merely an adjustment or reaction to the latest change in direction.

The last change in direction sends the side someplace that closes it. Remember, every side is a scene in a film, and every scene ends and the film cuts to someplace else, either in location or in time. For a story to progress the audience needs a clear understanding where things are at the *end* of a scene so that the next scene can progress the story by either *building* on that same direction or by being in *counter-point* to it. If you end your side with strong, clear choice, the Casting Director will see how your take on the side fits into the whole story. When Eleanor takes Clifton's drink she's doing more than just *taking a sip* of scotch. She's *reveling* in the fact that she's just taken over his world, all the way to the food and liquid he puts in his mouth. By having a strong choice at the end, we know exactly who Eleanor is at this moment and what the scene has done to her. Her journey is clear and the audience watching this scene in film can almost taste the conflicts that are to come.

A WORD ABOUT "BEATS"

I've heard many people, teachers, Casting Directors, actors, refer to what I am terming "change in direction" as beats. "Make sure you hit the beats" is an often-used phrase. I don't like the term "beats" because I feel it implies *stasis* or something that goes *bang* then just sits there. *Sitting there* is the exact opposite of what needs to happen in a side if it is to come alive. "Hitting a beat" doesn't give you anything to work with, doesn't give you any place to travel; "a change in direction" does. A change in direction gives you an opportunity to let what is happening in the side take you someplace else and it lets you experience the journey in any number of different ways. And during any *journey* you don't *stay still*.

SIZE DOES MATTER

I want to be very clear that by *strong* choices I do not necessarily mean *big or loud* choices. A strong choice is simply one that is clear, easy to understand, not ambivalent. Sometimes these choices are extremely subtle, a change inside you that produces a change in the eyes; a change that a camera will pick up, even if someone sitting five feet away may not. It isn't a big moment at the end of the Diner side when Jarrod tells Melinda it's nice to meet somebody like her, but it is a definite moment; both strangers have just taken a step towards a closer relationship. Jarrod by what he says and Melinda by how she reacts to it. Not a big, huge moment, but one that needs to happen.

Remember you are auditioning for a *film*. Not only is it possible that the finished film will be seen on a screen thirty feet high, films tend to employ close-ups much more frequently than television. Whatever choice you make, be sure that the delivery of that choice doesn't overshadow the choice itself.

WORKSHEET FOR FINDING CHOICES

Take any of the three scenes from chapter two, or choose one of your own.

1. What has happened in your life to bring you to this point? You can write as long and detailed description as you like in the beginning, but work on it to pare it down to one or two sentences. In paring it down, strengthen your verbs and adverbs so that in one or two sentences the emotional effect of what has happened to you is clear.

2. Why are you here? Whether you enter the scene on camera or are found already in the room or place, you came there for a reason. Just because it may happen off screen doesn't make it any less important. Did you come expecting a confrontation with another character or are you caught unawares by any information or attitude the other character brings?

3. What is the first thing you do? Is it something you *say* or something you *do*? What is your first choice? Does it embody everything you've discovered so far? Does it include the other character's anticipated reaction to your choice?

4. Where are the changes in direction? How do these changes affect you as you go through the scene? Reexamine them to make sure they are changes in direction and not merely adjustments. If they are true changes in directions, what choices go along with them?

5. How do you leave? What is the scene's final change in direction? Do you cause it or are you reacting to it? Does your final choice paint a clear and specific picture of where you are and how you feel at the end of the scene?

CHAPTER 4

EVEN MORE CHOICES

Now that you've made your choices and picked what seemed perfectly obvious, throw them away. I'm serious! Well, maybe don't throw them away, just put them aside. You're going to go through the entire side again.

As you go through it this time, purposely make choices that are the *exact opposite* of what you chose before. For example, if you made a choice in the Jarrod/Melinda side to be *anxious* to meet Melinda in person, pick the opposite, *dread* meeting her. Doesn't make any difference what the side says, what the dialogue says, what the action says. Go through the side and make opposite choices everywhere.

MOVE AROUND

When you physically move you free up your creativity in ways staying still cannot.

"What's going on," you ask? "I've just spent a lot of time carefully making choices and now you want me to make opposite choices?" Too many actors read a side and decide definitively what it's about. They make their choices and never think about them again. A side is rarely, if ever, exactly what you think it is. How you view a side is based on who you are, what your life experiences have been, what movies you've seen, what movies you'd like to see, what you hope you never see again, etc. That's how we're wired to make sense of the world. No matter what we encounter our brain processes it through our past experiences and presents us with a conclusion based on those experiences. This isn't necessarily a bad thing. It is what keeps us from getting mugged on a dark street or touching a flame. That's our brain's job, to take in the countless bits of information that accost us every second of every day and make order of it so we can proceed through the world in a manner best suited to who and what we are. So to make sure we're really *exploring all possibilities* in any material, we need to make sure we're not just taking the first -- or safest -- path that appears before us.

Making purposely *opposite* choices frees us to explore the life of a side in a completely different light. In every bit of real life there are multitudes of feelings, all the time. In any *loving* relationship there are moments of *irritation*, to put it nicely. With anyone you swear you *hate* there might possibly be buried somewhere down deep an iota of *respect*, compassion or at least understanding. Making opposite choices frees up those possibilities so that we don't automatically exclude them.

Now read the side out loud with the opposite choices. How does it feel experiencing the words and actions with opposite choices? Weird? Forced? Maybe a little bit good, or eye-opening in parts?

Go through the side again. This time, look at your original choices and see if having played the opposites alters the way you look at the sides' direction adjustments and changes. The altered view doesn't have to be dramatic. It could just be a minor shift. Did playing the opposite choices suggest a refinement of a particular choice or did it open up something new, a different way of looking at the change of direction that inspired the original choice? Instead of being simply *angry* at a particular point in the side, did exploring the opposite choice of *happy* produce a strong feeling of sarcasm? Did it make you feel the change of direction caused you more *frustration* than *anger*? If so, write the new choice down next to your original choice.

Look at all your choices again, the original ones as well as any you modified. Pick the one that speaks to you the strongest. If it's an original choice, use that as your first read. If it is another choice, or a combination of different choices, great. Use whatever feels the most right to you. If you present those choices in a clear and unambiguous manner, you can't go wrong.

A CHOICE IS NEVER *SET IN STONE*

Whatever choices you've made anywhere in the script, it is crucial that you keep yourself open to being affected by any other character's reaction to your choice. A choice is a *jumping off place*. It is what is going on with you as a result of what has just happened or what was just said. It is your reaction to the other character and the situation. In your preparing your side, you made choices based on how you felt a side seemed to progress. But what if it doesn't progress that way? What if, despite all the exclamation points, all CAPS and bold font that were written in the sides, what if the actor or Casting Director reading with you doesn't yell the dreadful words, "**I HATE YOU!**" and instead whispers them or breaks down into nearly silent tears or laughs? Whatever choice you made as to how you'd respond to that moment must be affected. If it isn't you've just taken yourself out of the scene and put yourself somewhere else. No matter what choices you've made, *everything* is up for grabs once the scene starts and you interact with another person.

Think of your own life. How many times have you been having an argument with someone and the other person starts laughing, or crying, or suddenly agrees with you that you're completely right? Did you just continue with whatever tirade you'd planned or did you react to them doing something you didn't expect? And even if you did try to continue with your tirade, needing to get out what you had to say, you know their reaction affected you in some way. The same is true in the audition. Whatever you've thought about how a side should go, it almost never goes that way without some deviation based on what the other person reading with you does.

"But what if I'm reading with a Casting Director who gives me nothing?"

This is probably the most frequent question I am asked by students with regard to being open to what you're given by a reader in an audition. I'd like to say that in the hundreds of audition rooms I've been in, almost never have I witnessed a reading by a Casting Director or reader in which *nothing* was given to the actor being auditioned. Sure, a reader may not be as plentiful and obvious with their reactions to your choices as a fellow actor might be. But if you're paying close attention you will get what they *are* giving.

Most times the Casting Director will read the sides the way he or she believes the director wants it to go, and as such, they will react accordingly to any choices you make.

If you listen to the words they say and are acutely sensitive to any inflection they give you, no matter how subtle, you'll get their intent. Your job is to then allow yourself to *react* to that intent and let it *affect* you and your next choice, no matter how subtly the intent may have been presented.

If you've done your work properly, if you've looked at the side from not only the viewpoint of your character but from the viewpoint of the writer telling a story, in most cases the way you see the sides will be very close to how a Casting Director sees it. There are exceptions, such as when you're given sides that are a small section of a much larger story and for various reasons you're given nothing about the larger story. But for most sides you're given, you have all the information you need to make the sensible choices the Casting Director expects you to make.

Most of the time the choices you have made in the sides will be fine, if you've made them with a clear understanding of the sides and if your choices themselves are clear. When you switch to a new choice based on the new direction the sides take, you'll be given an opportunity to see how your choice affected the person reading with you and that will either push you along the same choice or it might force you to modify it.

EXAMPLE:

In the Julie/Larry sides, when you, as Larry, decide to confess your affair, the Casting Director might read Julie's reaction with a *cry* in her voice. This must affect you differently than if she read it in *anger* or *disgust*, no matter what the line says.

In life, we never know how someone is going to react to something we say or do. We may have a good idea, but we're still frequently surprised.

In a story those surprises happen much more frequently than in real life, which is what makes a side *pop* when it's done well with strong choices. If you've made a choice in your work to attack a change in direction in the sides with the expectation that the person reading with you will rise to the attack and strike back but that person wilts and cries instead, you have to let that affect you. It might not change your whole choice from a blithering attack to becoming overwhelmed with heartfelt sympathy, but it must at least do *something* to you. If you have looked at the sides from different angles and explored the opposite of your original choices, you're going to be open and ready to react fully to anything the Casting Director or reader does. By exploring the sides from different angles you've released yourself from being locked into only one way of doing it.

If the choices you have made are *strong* it is so much easier to ride the wave of the side. *Strong choices produce strong reactions.* An audition filled with both is exciting to watch.

CHAPTER 5

TAKE A SIDE

PREPARING FOR A LEADING ROLE

Let's take an actual side and apply what we've discussed so far. For this example, I asked one of my students, Peter, to prepare as if he were auditioning for the lead, NEIL. I also asked several other students to prepare for the other roles as well, to see what they did with the same material, but reading for smaller roles. In this chapter we'll discuss Peter and his Prep Work for the lead role. This side begins on page 1 of the script.

```
INT. DARK, TOURISTY HOTEL BAR - ENSENADA-
NIGHT

The high-pitched SQUEAL of a mariachi
band singer PIERCES the air. A DANCER
swirls, her bright red dress flaring out
between two drunk American COLLEGE BOYS
who are desperately trying to dance with
her.
```

They both reach for her, but she sails
effortlessly out of the way, leaving them
stumbling into each other, laughing, as
their friends cheer them on.

Above the bar a sign reads:

"ENRIQUE AND LESLIE, SENOR Y SENORA AT
LAST!"

NEIL RENCHARD, 20s, holding a nearly finished margarita in his hand, looks around
the bar with thinly veiled disgust. BRYCE
HUTTON, 20s, sits next to him, dancing in
his chair. He lets out a WHOOP as the
dancer whips out castanets.

                    NEIL
          You like that noise?

                    BRYCE
          Hell yeah!

ENRIQUE, tall with steamy Latin-lover
looks and LESLIE, Malibu Barbie in a wedding dress, wrap themselves around each
other as they laugh and move to the music. The college boys clap as they dance.

                    COLLEGE BOYS
          Dip! Dip! Dip!

The rest of the bar takes up the chant, and Enrique clumsily lunges forward, dipping, and almost dropping, his bride. The crowd CHEERS as he brings her back up. Neil finishes his margarita. He grabs the arm of a Latina WAITRESS, as she walks by.

> NEIL
> Can I get another one?
> In a clean glass this
> time?

The Waitress, 20s, looks down her exquisitely chiseled nose at Neil. Her eyes seethe as she stares at Neil's hand on her arm. Neil lets go. She clenches her jaw and walks away. Bryce looks at Neil, shaking his head.

> NEIL (CONT'D)
> What?

> BRYCE
> Do you have to be such
> a bourgeois, American
> pig?

                    NEIL
Excuse me? Is it my
fault this whole coun-
try is a ghetto? I
don't know why Les-
lie's marrying this
jerk in the first
place. And in Mexico,
of all places on the
planet. Leslie's stom-
ach can't take any-
thing hotter than a
grape.

                    BRYCE
A, Enrique's hot as
Hell. B, he's Mexican,
and his parents did
pay for the wedding,
so…

                    NEIL
He's just marrying her
for a green card.

                    BRYCE
Whoa, bitter party of
one. You liked Enrique
when you were both on
the tennis team.

                    NEIL
Yeah, well that was
before.

                    BRYCE
          Besides, they met in
          this bar on Spring
          break. It's a wedding,
          where's your sense of
          romance?

                    NEIL
          In the toilet, thanks
          to the food.

The waitress walks up and plops a margarita down in front of Neil. Not looking
at her, Neil holds up a bill. She takes
the money, puts change on the table. Neil
looks at the change.

                    NEIL (CONT'D)
          I gave you a fifty.

                    WAITRESS
          You gave me a twenty.

She walks away, quickly winding through
the crowd.

                    NEIL
          Come back here!

Neil leaps up and pushes after her. He
reaches out and grabs her arm. WAITRESS
whips around and pushes Neil away.

                    WAITRESS
          Don't touch me!

                    NEIL
            You stole my money!

                  WAITRESS
            Get away from me!

A BOUNCER comes up.

                  BOUNCER
            What's going on?

                    NEIL
            She stole my money! I
            want to see the man-
            ager.

                  WAITRESS
                (in Spanish)
            He's a liar! He
            grabbed me.

The mariachis stop playing as everyone in
the bar focuses on Neil and the waitress.

                    NEIL
            Where's the manager?

The MANAGER, a distinguished Latino man
with black hair and grey temples, walks
up.

                  MANAGER
            What's the problem?

> NEIL
> I gave her a fifty and
> she gave me change for
> a twenty.

> WAITRESS
> That's a lie! He gave
> me a twenty.

> NEIL
> I gave you a fifty!
> You walked away with
> the change. You think
> you're worth that big
> a tip? For your shitty
> service?

The waitress SLAPS Neil across the face.

> MANAGER
> Geralda! You're fired.
> Leave, now!

The waitress glares at Neil, turns and
storms away.

> MANAGER (CONT'D)
> I'm sorry for the...
> shitty service.

> NEIL
> Yeah, well, it was.

Everyone in the bar stares at Neil, most
with barely hidden contempt. Leslie and
Neil lock eyes for a moment. Leslie
shakes her head and turns away.

```
                    NEIL (CONT'D)
          I gotta pee.

     Neil pushes his way out of the bar.
```

Before you read any further, take this side and go through it as you would if you were reading for the part of Neil. Doesn't make any difference if you're a man or woman, the Prep Work is still the same.

Peter read with another student who read as the Casting Director.

KEVIN: Peter, tell me about the work you did on the sides, your breakdown.

PETER: It all seemed pretty obvious to me.

WHERE – In a bar in Mexico, dirty.

WHEN – Night, after a wedding.

WHAT – I'm complaining about the bar and the service.

WHO – Neil, guy who's probably a bit racist, pissed to be here, not having a good time.

WHY – For Neil, he just wants a drink in a clean glass and a waitress who doesn't steal his money! For the story – the scene happens to take Neil from one location to another.

KEVIN: Ok. That's pretty bare bones.

PETER: Well it's the first page of the script, so there's not really a whole lot going on yet. The dialogue is pretty straight forward.

KEVIN: Yes it's the beginning, but as the beginning, there's a ton of information in this side. It's setting up the entire story.

PETER: Yeah, but I didn't have any other information about the story or character except this side. You didn't give us a breakdown.[1]

KEVIN: You don't need a breakdown. Sure it's nice when you get them, but more often than not you don't get them, which makes it all that more important to read the sides carefully. In this case, you really don't need a breakdown. These sides are all you need. Let's look them together. Take your WHERE. Yes, it's a bar in Mexico.

PETER: A dirty bar.

KEVIN: Why do you say that?

PETER: Neil asks for a drink in a *clean* glass.

KEVIN: Yes he does. Is there any other indication, anywhere else in the side that says it's a dirty bar?

PETER: No, but he says it for a reason.

KEVIN: Exactly. I'm not saying ignore that very important bit of information, but before you assign it meaning, you have to look at the whole scene. This is not just a bar in Mexico. The writer has created a very specific place, visually and audibly. The bar is described as being "Dark, Touristy Hotel Bar – Ensenada." Look at that description carefully. Ensenada is not a little village off in the middle of the country nor is it Mexico City. It's a seaside tourist resort. This one is a hotel bar, even more dependent on tourists for income. And it's a hotel bar that can afford to hire a band and at least one dancer, a good dancer at that since the writer describes her as "sailing effortlessly" out of the way of a couple of drunken college boys. So it's not a dive. But before that, the first impression the writer gives you that will hit the audience as the film opens is the "high-pitched SQUEAL of a mariachi band." See the caps he used for SQUEAL? That tells you the scene is starting off with a BANG of noise.

---

[1] A breakdown is a character description and brief synopsis of the plot as it affects the character, most often prepared by Breakdown Services, Ltd.

PETER: But Neil thinks it's a dump.

KEVIN: He does, but it's an opinion that doesn't appear to be shared by either the writer or any of the other characters in the side, so that's an important bit of information that cannot be ignored. The WHERE of this side is in incredibly important as it not only sets up the location, it sets up Neil as someone who is out of step with everyone else. If you just dismiss it as a dirty bar, you're missing everything the writer took great pains to give you. To *Neil* it may be just that, but not to anyone else. To Enrique and Leslie it's where they're celebrating their wedding. To their college friends it's a place with music and dancers that have them whooping and cheering. So it's a place full of life to everyone except Neil.

In your WHEN, yes it is night and after a wedding but it's so much more than that. It's when everyone *except* Neil is having a good time. Does Neil think this marriage was a good idea?

PETER: No.

KEVIN: So it's after a wedding/celebration has taken place. A wedding Neil didn't think was a good idea. It's also after many people in the scene have had a lot to drink. Neil has had at least one drink, maybe more. There's a lot more that can go into this *When*, but we'll come back to that when we look at your *Why*. So, with this expanded *Where* and *When*, do you want to look at your Who again? Read what you wrote then see if you want to change it now?

PETER: I wrote "a guy who's probably a bit racist, pissed to be here, not having a good time." I think it's the same. Everyone else is having a good time; he's not, so he hates Mexico.

KEVIN: He does seem to, at least at this point. Let's take a closer look at the sides to see if we can find more information. But before we go any further, let me warn all of you about writing something like "he's probably a bit racist." Folks, this is *your* work, *your* take on this side, so don't use words like "probably." How do you play that? What does a non-specific, wishy-washy word like "probably" do for you except give you an excuse not to make a decision? *Make a definite decision.* If it's not correct based on information you find out later, fine. Then you make another one. But if your decisions about any part of the *Where, When,* and *Who* are not definite and specific, any choice you make won't be definite and specific either. Your choices will be weak and confusing to anyone watching your work.

Let's look at the sides again. Doesn't Neil say that the bride, Leslie, can't eat hot food? Doesn't he disparage the marriage as a sham so that Enrique can get a green card? And doesn't Bryce accuse Neil of liking Enrique when they were on the tennis team? What does that say to you about Neil? It tells me he knows Leslie intimately enough to know her digestive system, liked Enrique when they were buds, but now that he's Leslie's husband doesn't like him or his country. Tells me that Neil and Leslie were a couple at one time or at least that he had a thing for her. Doesn't that in turn give the *When* and *Where* whole different colors? It's now a place *Where* his probable ex is celebrating her marriage to someone else, someone who appears to be Neil's opposite. It's *When* all that is being rubbed in loudly and celebrated by everyone else around him. So now Neil is not necessarily a racist, but more likely a man in pain, a man for whom everything that has to do with this marriage, from the glass in his hand to the entire country, is a slap in the face.

PETER: I didn't see all that but I do now.

KEVIN: This is why I tell you all to read every word in the sides very carefully. You're about to take a journey and the sides are your only roadmap. You can't afford to miss any bit of information that is written. You have to take all the two dimensional words you're given and combine them in order to turn them into a three dimensional world.

Would you like to revisit your *Why?*

PETER: I sure do. I think now, for Neil, he's in a place he doesn't want to be, a place that, as you pointed out, is giving him pain. So he's, I don't know, trying to deal with this the best he can until he can't take it anymore and he has to get out.

KEVIN: I like that. Do you see how much more interesting and compelling Neil's experience of these sides is with that description as compared with what you wrote earlier, "He just wants a drink in a clean glass and a waitress who doesn't steal his money." Those things are important because they are what he latches on to in the sides to express himself. But does he only want a clean glass or is he asking for a clean life without any problems and demands that someone else bring it to him? That may sound a little artsy but that doesn't mean it's not true. He doesn't want a waitress to steal his money but he also doesn't want Enrique to steal his girl. And since, for whatever reasons, Neil doesn't or didn't have the ability to share all this concern with Leslie and Enrique before they got married (if he did I doubt he'd be here), he is taking out his frustration and pain on what and who is available; a glass and a waitress. Not to say she didn't steal his money, as the sides don't clarify that. But even if she did, it is clear that this part of the scene is an extension of Neil's belief that Enrique stole his girl. Now you have a *Who* and *Why* that are so much richer and all that from merely reading the side more carefully.

Now let's look at your choices. I have to say that your reading was a little flat, one dimensional. I'm sure it's because your choices were based on the flat and one dimensional view of the sides you had before we looked at it together. But, tell me your first choice.

PETER: I can't believe the guy next to me, Bryce, likes the noise of this bar.

KEVIN: That's your first choice? That is the first thing that you do in this side?

PETER: Yeah, I'm the first one to speak. I'm just sitting in the bar.

KEVIN: Yes you are, but the writer has created a very specific place and given you a very specific reaction to this place. In your reading, nothing happened with you until you spoke. But that is not the first thing you do in this side. In your line, you're commenting on the noise of the mariachi band and probably on the whole place as well. So the first thing that happens to you, according to what is written in these sides, is that you *hear the noise, see the band, dancers, everyone else having a good time*, including probably the only friend you have in the place. You totally missed your first choice which is *to register how this place is affecting you*. Doesn't need to be big, you don't need to hold ears and squint at the loud music, but you do need to take a moment to hear and see all the stuff happening all around you and let it affect you. This is a major *change in direction* in the script, as the writer has set up a world where everyone is having fun until we see you. Then you missed your second choice, which was to take another moment to *recognize that your friend actually likes it.* THEN you speak. This is why the reading was flat when it began. You were relying on the *words* to set the scene, when what we needed was your *reaction* to everything going on to set it. You gave me nothing until you spoke, even though the camera was filming you before you spoke. What was your choice?

PETER: It was like, disbelief.

KEVIN: Again, a non-definite, non-specific choice. "Like disbelief."

PETER: I didn't write "like" I wrote "disbelief."

KEVIN: Maybe you did, but the fact that you described your choice as "like disbelief" means that is how this choice affected you; in a general, wishy-washy way. Like disbelief, but maybe like some other things too. But, going with *disbelief*, can anyone tell me how you play disbelief? What do you do, open your eyes real wide, open your mouth and stare?

The class laughs.

KEVIN: What you wrote down is a word that doesn't say anything. That's not a choice as much as a thought. How about something a bit more personal? Just off the top of my head, "I don't want to be here, I can't even be depressed in peace with the noise of this crappy band, and I'm tired of suffering in silence so I'm going to take it out on my friend next me so I can vent." See how much more personally unique that is? Notice the strong words I used; *Depressed, Noise, Crappy, Suffering, Take it Out, Vent*. Also, you're in a loud bar. But you began so quietly, you wouldn't be heard by anyone standing a foot away from you.

PETER: Yeah, but I wanted to be really present right now with what is actually going on.

KEVIN: That's fine, but you can't ignore the facts of the story. I know there is no noise here but there may not be any on the set either. Many times they add the music and crowd noises in post-production so they can get clean dialogue. But you'd have to film the scene *as if* all the noise was happening. You need to show the Casting Director you understand the sides and what is going on. By reading it as if you were sitting in a quiet room next to someone, you were putting yourself in a different scene. And it affected your performance as well. Because you started off with a weak choice, the read never got to a place that showed me anything unique about you. You just came across as a guy who was generally in a bad mood.

PETER: Actually, that's kind of how I felt during the reading.

KEVIN: Do you see how all that you did came together to produce a weak reading?

PETER: Yeah. I guess I need to read the sides a lot more carefully.

KEVIN: Good idea.

PETER: But, I also am afraid of being too big, too much. You keep hearing Casting Directors say, "don't act, be real."

KEVIN: Exactly, *be real with what's going on in the sides*. But I'm glad you brought this up. There is this widespread fear among Film and Television actors that if they're not "real" they'll be accused of "acting" or "overacting." So yeah, they're real... real boring. First of all, most actors don't even know what a Casting Director means when he says "be real." They think it means act like you do in real life which translates to: be nice, even-keeled, low energy, just sit or stand there and talk like you would any normal moment of the day in your real life. WRONG. What is meant by "be real" is act as if everything carefully written in the sides is *real to you* at that moment. Any Film or Television show is a story, *it is not real life*; it is *life concentrated*. For most stories it would be impossible for everything that happens in the film to take place in an hour and a half. In a film like *Twelve Years A Slave*, it happens over twelve years! And yet the director, writer and actors had only about two hours or so to tell that story. So everything in every scene of any film is a *concentration of life*.

Take your sides. In real life just that specific scene would most likely take place over a couple of hours. Neil would sit there for some time, stewing about everything that has happened before it gets to the point where he vents by insulting the waitress, which gets him slapped, gets everyone in the bar to stare at him with disgust to which he responds by leaving. And that says nothing about all the time it would have taken in real life *before* the scene even begins to set things in motion. All the time Neil spent dating or at least knowing Leslie, the time during Leslie's engagement to Enrique, and so forth. But everything that happens in the sides, even though in real life it would have taken hours, takes approximately four minutes, based on a page of a film script equaling a minute of film time. *Four minutes* to go through what, in real life, would have taken hours. The only way for a writer to create a scene that does that is to get to the *changes in direction* as quickly as possible and to make them as clear and strong as possible. The actor must also do the same, understand where the scene goes and make clear, strong choices that take it there during the few minutes it takes to go through the sides. Remember all sides are a journey. Some are longer than others, but it is a journey, one that in real life would probably take much longer than the length of the sides. So you have to make strong choices otherwise the journey doesn't happen.

PETER: I understand all that but I'm always afraid, especially during a first audition, of coming off too strong. What if I'm all wrong about how the sides are supposed to go?

KEVIN: Then you're wrong and the Casting Director will give you whatever information or direction he can to get you on the right track. But you have to give him something strong and definite so he knows where you are. If you make weak choices, you're not being real, you're just being vague. A Casting Director would have no idea whether you didn't understand the sides or were just unable to make a clear choice. All he knows is that the reading was flat. If you give him strong choices, the choices may be wrong based on information you did not get or have interpreted incorrectly, but at least the Casting Director knows where you stand and has an idea of how to re-direct you. Chances are he can impart what he wants to see from you with anywhere from a few words to a full sentence. But if you give him weak and unclear choices, he won't know where to begin to help you.

Do you think most Casting Directors would take the time I've just spent with you to get you on the right track? They have too many other actors to read. So help them by making strong choices, then playing them in as real a manner as you can, based on all the specifics of the *Where, When, Who* and *What* of the sides.

Peter, with your new, clearer understanding of the Where, When, What and Who of your side, do you want to re-examine your first choices in this side?

PETER: Let's see… my first choice is my reaction to the music. Easy, because I hate loud bars, so all I have do is be myself, hating the loud music. Then I look over at my friend, and there he is, *liking* it. Not only that, he's my friend, he knows all I've been through with Leslie, how can he ignore all that and not see how everything here is making me feel? I feel a little betrayed by him, like he's taking Leslie's side over mine.

KEVIN: Excellent. Now you're beginning the sides with a definite point of view, a definite set of personal reactions to what is going on. If the Casting Director wants you to be more or less upset, angry or whatever you give based on how you're affected by these choices, at least you're giving him a *definite position*, something *solid* to either accept or redirect. If your choice is strong there is no doubt about how you feel.

GO OVER YOUR DISSECTIONS AGAIN

Look back at your *Where, When, What* and *Who*. Are they specific enough? Do they include everything that the writer has put down or did you generalize? Redo them if you need, making sure they reflect *all* that is going on in the side.

Now look at your choices. Did you also start with the first dialogue or did you start with Neil's reaction to the music? If you expanded your *Where, When, What*, and *Who*, do you want to revisit your original choices so that they reflect those expansions? Are they strong, meaning are they *clear* and *definite*, or are they vague? Do your choices evoke specific and strong feelings in you? If they don't, refine them until they do.

CHAPTER 6

PREPARING FOR A FILM SUPPORTING ROLE

Now that you've looked at the sides from Neil's perspective, let's look at them as if you're going to read for a smaller part. I asked several other students to prepare the parts of Bryce, the Waitress and the Manager.

David prepared the part of Bryce. His reading was good, a lot of energy, but not as focused as it could have been.

KEVIN: Good. David tell me about your work on the side. Give me everything but your *Why* for now.

DAVID:

WHERE - in a bar in Mexico with a great band.

WHEN - after my friends' wedding.

WHAT – I'm enjoying the band, having a good time. Neil is complaining about everything, being a real pain in the ass.

WHO – I'm a guy having a good time at a wedding.

KEVIN: Ok. Before I discuss this work further, tell me your first choice.

DAVID: I'm responding to Neil asking me if I like the music.

KEVIN: Really? I think the first choice begins before that. Read the action paragraph again.

> BRYCE HUTTON, 20s, sits next to him,
> dancing in his chair.
>
> He lets out a WHOOP as the dancer whips
> out castanets.

So you actually start the scene dancing in your chair and let out a "whoop." Now I'm not saying you have to give a Tarzan yell but you do have to be into the music so much that it prompts Neil to ask you about it. Every scene in a film is about the relationship of the characters involved and their interaction with each other. That is what propels a scene forward, leading to the next scene. If you don't start this scene by visibly enjoying yourself to the point where it forces Neil to say something, then there is no scene.

DAVID: Yeah, I guess so. I just took it for granted, you know, with the loud music and stuff that he'd be annoyed enough to say something.

KEVIN: He might, but why talk to you? Why not just yell at the band to shut up? His dialogue is very specific; he asks if *you* like the music. So you have to at least appear to like it before he says anything or the scene will never even begin. It also will give you a point of focus. Your reading was full of nice energy but it didn't seem to be connected to anything in the scene. You were just sitting on the edge of your seat and being super attentive to Neil. If you take all that great energy and allow it to be present in response to the music, you create a situation where you are in one world and Neil has to constantly try to drag you out of it and into his world. It also allows you to use your energy to try to lure Neil into your world.

I like your WHERE, WHEN and WHAT, but your WHO is a little weak.

DAVID: It doesn't really say much about Bryce, just that he's having a good time.

KEVIN: I think it says quite a lot about Bryce. For one thing, he's mostly likely gay.

DAVID: Where does it say that?

KEVIN: He refers to Enrique, Leslie's new husband, as "hot as Hell." Not too many straight guys call each other "hot as Hell." So the writer didn't say Bryce was gay in his description, he showed us in Bryce's behavior and dialogue. Now, that doesn't mean you have to run around playing a ridiculous stereotype, but it will give you a more insight as to who Bryce is.

Now, tell me *Why* is this scene happening from the perspective of the story? What is the purpose of Bryce even being in this scene from that perspective?

DAVID: It shows us Neil's in a bad place, personally. And Bryce being there gives him someone to talk to, I guess confide in a bit.

KEVIN: Yes it does. Secondary characters' purposes are to *flesh out* the main characters, especially in a scene like this. Bryce's purpose is to listen to Neil and challenge him, pushing him along his journey. Without Bryce, Neil would probably just get up and leave. But he doesn't, he bounces his feelings off Bryce. Bryce, in turn, doesn't let him get away with complaining, he challenges Neil. Not only does this give the audience exposition, explaining a bit of what has happened to make Neil feel this way, it sets up Neil as someone who is alone in feeling the way he feels. So alone that he acts out and creates a scene and finally storms out of the bar. Bryce helps this happen by being a friend who is close enough to Neil that Neil feels comfortable speaking openly of his disdain for Leslie's marriage and the bar, but also close enough that he doesn't let Neil get away with feeling sorry for himself.

Bryce also gives us hope for Neil. Bryce seems like a nice guy who sees something worthwhile in Neil. If he didn't, he would just dismiss Neil or get up and move away. He doesn't. He stays and despite Neil trying to make Bryce hate the whole place as much as he does, Bryce remains solid in his feelings, challenging Neil without pushing him away. We challenge people we care for; we push away those we don't. So if Bryce sees value in Neil it tells the audience that there is value buried under all his crap. So in portraying Bryce be a friend, someone who accepts the good and urges Neil to rethink the bad. Someone who challenges Neil gently enough that Neil can still complain, but someone who won't blindly accept Neil's crap so that Neil has to take his frustration out on the waitress.

DAVID: Wow, I just looked at it as a couple of buds in a bar after at a wedding.

KEVIN: Exactly. And that is why your reading, though good, wasn't focused. You were there, talking and reacting to Neil, but you weren't really pushing back. You weren't helping him along his journey.

I'd like you to read the scene again, allowing the notes I gave you to affect you in some way.

David's second reading of the same scene was much more focused. He responded to the "music" at the start, which gave his interaction with Neil much more power. He was having such a good time dancing in his chair that it was a great counter-balance to Neil's opposite reaction to the whole place. And he didn't do anything overtly "gay" but when he read the line about Enrique being "hot as Hell" he had a little sparkle in his eye that was missing the time before. Nothing big, but it was there and it served to create a fuller character.

David's portrayal of Bryce more actively challenged Neil the second time. He was a good friend who wouldn't let him get away with sinking into depression. His energy was focused on the music at first, then on trying to poke and prod Neil into getting out of his funk. Bryce's journey in the scene was much clearer, going from a guy *enjoying* the music while sitting next to his friend to *challenging* his friend's statements and beliefs. This made Neil's journey that much clearer and the scene moved in a definite direction.

The two actors reading the Waitress and the Manager, Beth and Jason, did fine, but Beth was a little too strong and forceful in her reading. Let me explain what I mean by that.

KEVIN: Beth tell me about your work, including your *Why*.
BETH:
WHERE - the hotel bar where I work.
WHEN - at night with a bunch of rowdy, snobby Americans.
WHAT - a typical American jerk accuses me of giving him a dirty glass then of stealing his money. He grabs me, I slap him then I get fired.
WHO - I'm a waitress, I don't steal and I'm sick and tired of all the crap the American tourists give me.
WHY – I'm not going to let anyone treat me the way Neil does, accuse me of something I didn't do and physically assault me.
KEVIN: All right. Good, but you didn't give me a Why from the perspective of the story. I know your character is smaller but that is when it is the *most important* to the story *Why*.

Beth, you created a full person, very opinionated and strong. The trouble is, if you had done the *Why* from the perspective of the story, you would see how that doesn't work for this scene. There is a rule that the *smaller the character, the more specific his or her reason for being in the script must be*. Writers don't just add characters to fill up space. There is a reason for every character and that reason is to further the story. The smaller the role the less time there is to move the story, so you have to be very clear about how a small role moves the story and how a small role contributes to the main characters' journeys.

By being so opinionated from the beginning you are like Neil in that you have stereotyped people. To you, all Americans are pains in the asses. That may be true but your obvious dislike of Neil from the very beginning makes it less offensive to the audience when Neil accuses you of giving him a dirty glass and stealing money. If you come across as disliking Americans, no matter who they are, it makes it quite believable that you would do the things Neil accuses you of. If the audience thinks that you did these things, then Neil is quite justified in his reaction to you and there is no reason for him to feel embarrassed and storm out of the bar.

You're working in a bar dependent upon tourists for your income and tips. The better waitress you are, regardless of who your clientele is or how you feel about them personally, the more money you will make. But more importantly, if you look at the script from the point of finding the main character's journey, you will see how your character has to come across in order to help him with that journey. You don't have to like the way Neil treats you, in fact you hate it so much you hit him, but it has to be clear that Neil is overreacting, that Neil and only Neil feels that you're giving him dirty glasses and stealing his money. If you have an "I-hate-all-Americans" attitude, that hinders Neil's journey instead of helping him along it. By being a good waitress or at least a less overtly hostile waitress, you create doubt in the audience's mind regarding Neil's accusations.

BETH: But I figured he'd been treating me that way all night.

KEVIN: Where in the scene does it say that?

BETH: It doesn't say that specifically but by his attitude I assumed it.

KEVIN: Why couldn't you assume that he only became belligerent as he became drunker? Why couldn't you assume that he has sat at the bar depressed most of the night? Your assumption that he's been rude to you all night made you approach him already wary and disrespectful of him, which in turn gives his treatment of you some justification. This doesn't further his journey it blocks it and confuses it. If you approach him in a friendlier, or at least professional manner, it makes it obvious he's the bad guy here.

KEVIN: Ok, Jason tell me about your work.

JASON:

WHERE - at the hotel bar where I work.

WHEN - at night when the bar is full with a bunch of Americans.

WHAT - one of the customers complains about a waitress, she slaps him and I fire her.

WHO - I'm the manager of there restaurant, I'm doing my job.

WHY - from my perspective, I need to intervene to resolve a customer's dispute, and definitely need to intervene when my employee hits a customer. Bad for business if I don't!

Jason, you did seem to understand the *WHY* from the story's perspective. Did you work on it?

JASON: Yes. My story *WHY* is that because of him and his bad attitude he's to blame for everything. I want to embarrass him in front of the whole bar.

KEVIN: Exactly! His being embarrassed is what makes him storm out. So your understanding of the *WHY* from the story's perspective gave your reading the edge that made it clear to Neil and everyone around him that you were going to behave in a professional and respectful manner even though he did not. Your specific reason for being in the story is this moment, as it is what leads to Neil leaving the bar and journeying/moving to the next scene.

I want to say it again, it is *essential* to discover how supporting characters move the story along in the specific way the writer intended. Nothing Beth did was "wrong" in terms of playing a character in this environment, but her aggressive attitude interfered with the writer's intentions as her attitude made it appear that Neil might have had a very good reason to talk to her the way he did. Her attitude made Neil the victim instead of the aggressor, which isn't what is written. By looking at the scene from the perspective of the main character's journey, you can see how a supporting role fits in and how to best help the main character's journey instead of hindering it.

WATCH FILMS, paying attention to the supporting characters. Really analyze how they move the story along, how they aid the main characters' journeys. When reading for a supporting role in a film it is imperative you discover the story *Why* for any scene your character is in. Really be able to define what happens in any supporting role's interaction with any other character and *how* that interaction furthers the main character's journey.

CHAPTER 7

THE ONE OR TWO LINE FILM AUDITION

In many films there are one or two line character parts. These can be the most challenging auditions for many actors.

"What can I do with one line?" or "There isn't anything there to really sink my teeth into." "How do I make an audition for a part this small memorable?"

These are the complaints I hear constantly when coaching actors for auditions. To solve this dilemma, let's examine these parts and discover what the Producers and Casting Directors are looking for when auditioning these parts.

YES, THERE ARE SMALL PARTS

Writers create one or two line parts for a reason. No, it's not to tease or insult actors. Every character, every word of dialogue in a script takes time and nowhere is the old saying "Time is Money" more true than in shooting a film. So if a scene has a one or two line character in it, that character is there for a very good reason.

We've discussed how a film's story is about the main character's or characters' journeys. A writer will create one or two line roles because the story needs a little something at that moment to help *define the world* of the journey or journeys. Think of a one or two line role like seasoning in a stew; a pinch of this, a smidgen of that, all work together to bring out the full flavor of the dish. Leave out one or more of the seasonings and the dish falls flat.

DO YOUR PREP

Just because a role only has one or two lines you still have to do your Prep. You need to know the Where, What, When, Who and Why of your character just as much as you would if you were reading for the lead; sometimes *even more so*, because you have only one or two lines to fit into the story.

A PART OF THE WORLD

A one or two line character appears as a normal part of the story's world at that moment and is created for two reasons.

   1- To fill out the world of the story at that moment.
   2- To represent the relationship of the world to the main
      character or characters at that moment.

These roles fill out the world of the story by populating it. These roles are most frequently people the main character or characters would encounter briefly in everyday life; store clerks, strangers on the street, food servers, bus drivers, anybody who would populate the world of the story at that point. Very few stories take place in a vacuum, so a writer needs people to populate his world.

But in addition to populating the story's world a one or two line role represents the *relationship of this world* to the main character or characters at that point. At any point in a story the main character or characters are *in sync* with their world or *in conflict* with it. The one or two line character helps define either situation. The friendly waitress who greets a main character with a cheery, "Good morning, want your usual?" is part of a much different world than one where a stranger on the streets bumps into the same main character and snarls, "Watch where you're going, jerk!" In both cases these characters are normal inhabitants of their world but both have vastly different relationships with a main character. The writer created each role to show the relationship between a main character and a smaller character because that relationship mirrors the relationship that main character has with his or her world at that point.

KNOW YOUR WORLD

In auditioning for a one or two line role, know your world. Is it one where you normally have control? If you're at work, whatever the job, chances are you have a modicum of control. In the case of the friendly waitress, she not only has control, it is a world where everything is fine. In the case of the stranger on the street, he is not at work but is still in a world where he feels a degree of control or at least wants to feel in control which is why he snaps at the character who bumps into him instead of apologizing.

KNOW YOUR PURPOSE

Why is this role here at this point in the story? Is it to be in harmony with a main character or in conflict?

"What can I do with one line?"

Don't *do* anything; simply be a part of the story's world at that moment. That's doing enough. Whether your character is in harmony with a main character or is in conflict, it is a brief encounter because the writer wants a *quick* definition or reinforcement of a main character's relationship with his or her world.

"There isn't anything in one or two lines to sink my teeth into."

Sink your teeth into the simple and fine-tuned focus of whatever it is your character is doing at that moment.

"How do I make an audition for this part memorable?"

Your job isn't to be "memorable," or to stand out and apart from the story's world.

Your job is to represent that world as simply as possible. By trying to "make a big impression, or be a really memorable actor," you will most likely eclipse the purpose of the role and hijack the story.

If you bring too large a character to the role just because you want to do something interesting, you won't be *representing* the world of the story, but will be *presenting* your own world. That doesn't mean one or two line roles can't be full of interest and/or character, if that is the world the writer has created at that moment. But you must be an accurate representation of the story's world and size your performance accordingly.

Almost always, in film, *Simple is Best*.

CHAPTER 8

TELEVISION

The Television audition is a very close relative to the film audition. But in the

Television audition it is the *story* that is the focus rather than the specific journey of the main characters. The main characters do indeed have journeys but they are told over the course of a season rather than the course of an hour and a half or so that is the length of a typical film. The guest characters, Guest Stars, Co-Stars or Featured Actors, have journeys as well but their journeys vary in size with the biggest going to the Guest Stars and proceeding in descending order from Co-Stars to Featured.

TYPE OF TELEVISION SHOWS

EPISODICS

Episodics are generally an hour long. They are usually Dramatic in nature but are not limited to Dramas. *Glee* is an example of an Episodic that has drama and comedy and musical numbers.

Episodics have a core cast of Regular Characters. These Regular Characters are confronted with a problem each week, or episode, and usually solve it by the end of the episode unless it is a multi-episode arc.

However, many Episodics have a main story that runs the length of the season and though each episode presents a new problem, there is still a continuation of the main problem that is carried over from the episode or episodes before. An example of this type of Episodic might be a law-enforcement environment where the goal of the entire season might be to catch a particular criminal. Each episode might include a side story but most events in any given episode will be part of the larger story to catch the main criminal.

THE PROCEDURAL

A Procedural is a sub-genre of the Episodic and generally refers to law-enforcement or medical shows where each episode follows a typical *procedure* in order to tell the story.

A Law Enforcement Procedural will have a crime that is committed followed by the standard procedures employed to solve the crime. There will be an investigation, suspects brought in and questioned, arrests made, etc.

A Medical Procedural will be similar in that the story will generally follow a pattern. Someone gets sick, they get tested by the staff, their case will confound the medical professionals in whatever locale the show takes place and by the end the patient either gets better or dies.

A Legal Procedural is one where the story is set in a law firm or courthouse. Most episodes will revolve around the stories and procedures native to these environments.

In all Procedurals most episodes will follow the specific procedural patterns of their world in various ways. When reading for a Procedural it is important to recognize whether the story is told through the normal procedures or whether it strays from those, and if it does, how. There will be personal problems of the regular characters thrown in from time to time but the main focus of most episodes will be to solve the main problem, be it criminal or medical or legal.

These are just a few of the most prominent examples of Procedurals. When reading for a show, examine it carefully. Does it follow any particular set of procedures each episode that is germane to a particular profession no matter what the environment? Does it have its own unique language, i.e. legal, medical, military or law enforcement? If any of these apply, chances are it's a Procedural, and as such you must be familiar and comfortable with the language and the procedures involved in the world of the show, unless you are reading for a character who is an obvious outsider. Many an actor has lost a part because he mispronounced a medical or legal term in a Procedural audition.

DRAMAS

Though Procedurals are generally dramas not all Dramas are Procedurals. A non-Procedural Drama is one where the story or stories are dramatic in nature but do not follow any set of particular job-related procedures. It could be centered around a family or a group of people who find themselves involved in dilemmas each episode and the story focuses on their attempts to resolve these dilemmas.

THE SINGLE CAMERA COMEDY

The Single Camera Comedy is one that is *not* filmed in front of a live audience with several cameras, or one that *does not include a laugh track* after every joke. It is filmed much like an Episodic in that generally only one camera angle is shot at a time, with each scene performed many times, depending on the number of camera angles the Director wants. Though there may be recurring themes, generally a Single Camera Comedy has new problems confronting the regular characters each episode that are almost always resolved by the end of the episode. Hanging dilemmas are seldom funny and the goal of all comedies is to make the audience laugh. A problem may seem to be resolved only to rise again in a future episode, but by the end of each episode most loose ends are seemingly tied up.

THE SIT-COM

A Sit-Com, short for Situation Comedy, is generally three or more cameras filmed in front of a live audience or made to appear that way. The Sit-Com is presented much like a play in that each scene is filmed straight-through with stops only occurring if there is a problem. And though almost every comedic story is situational in that everything is proceeding nicely until something happens to disrupt things, the styles of Sit-Com and Single Camera Comedy are very different. I'll go into the specific differences in the sections devoted to the Sit-Com and the Single Comedy audition.

THE RE-ENACTMENT SHOW

A very popular type of show on Television is the Re-enactment show. In this type of program actors re-enact a real or made-to-appear real event or events. Most times these stories are dramatic in nature though there are some Re-enactment shows that are comedic.

CHAPTER 9

THE EPISODIC SERIES REGULAR LEAD AUDITION

THE SERIES REGULAR Audition is probably one of the most daunting auditions imaginable. You are being asked to demonstrate to legions of people that you will be able to hold an audience's attention week after week. Who are these legions of people? They include the Casting Director, the Producer(s), the Studio Exec(s), the Network Exec(s), the Writer and the Director, to name just a few. Depending on the series, the network, the studio or the budget, there could be many more involved. Let's just say you have to please a small crowd. Oh my God! How do you do that? How do you be everything to everybody?

First, banish that thought immediately. You can't be *everything* to *everybody*; ever. But what you can do is be *something* to everybody. And that *something* is *you*.

As a Series Regular you are going to be someone the audience becomes intimate with. Your job is to bring them into your world every week as they watch you navigate the ins and outs, ups and downs of this world; *week after week*. I am emphasizing week after week to make sure you understand that unlike a film where the audience spends an hour and a half on average with you, as a Series Regular you're going to be in people's living rooms up to an hour a week for as long as the season lasts. On Network television that is as few as 10 weeks and as long as 24 weeks.

Auditioning for a Series Regular is much like auditioning for a film. Your journey will be smaller than if you were only appearing in one episode, as it will be designed to last an entire season. Each episode is a section of that journey, one that will add to sections already seen in previous episodes and to sections in episodes yet to be filmed. Therefore your journey each week is small and takes a back seat to the story. This does not mean that the weekly journey of a Series Regular is unimportant; it means it is a journey that is drawn out over the course of a season. Some weeks it might seem to be stagnant, other weeks it might take a leap forward. But in Television the story is paramount and it is through the story that audiences experience the Series Regular's journey.

Each week, as a Series Regular, you will be confronted with problems you need to solve, or attempt to solve. Though you will almost always remain in your own world (the world of the show), the Guest Star will come in to disrupt that world. Your job is to get everything back on track as best you can. I like to think of the Series Regular as a ball in a game. The ball can be sent all over the field constantly in short bursts, like in soccer, or it can be sent flying a long way but with fewer hits, like in golf. It might be scuffed or chipped by the end of the game but is still round and fairly intact at the end, ready for the next game.

The story is the *path the ball takes* to eventually land in the goal or hole. The Guest Stars are the players kicking the ball or golfers hitting it with clubs to send it along the story path. Depending how hard the ball is kicked or struck, the ball will react accordingly.

The Series Regular is the audiences' guide, their leader. Whatever the world of your show you need to find, deep down inside of you, your unique ability to survive whatever your world will throw at you each week and come out relatively unscathed. You need to bring to the table a sense of *confidence* and *permanence*. That confidence may be bold and brash or quiet and subtle, but it is necessary to let the audience feel you are trustworthy and safe to follow each week.

When a new show goes into production, the first couple of seasons are fairly well mapped out before the first day of shooting. All the scripts aren't written as yet, but the Producers have a pretty good idea where they are going for the first three years and each show is conceived and written to eventually get there.

WHERE IN THE WORLD AM I?

It is imperative you know the type of story the new series will be or if you're reading for an existing series, what type of story the series is. Is it one that is designed so that each episode can be full and complete on its own or is it the type of show that will spend an entire season on one storyline, with each week's episode adding pieces to the puzzle? Shows that produce stand-alone episodes create a different journey for the Series Regulars than ones that pick up the story from the last week's episode and lead it to the next week's episode. In stand-alone shows the journey is fairly complete as most, if not all, of the conflicts and problems of the story will be resolved by the episode's end. In a show where each episode is a continuation of a larger journey each episode will not be complete, but one that picks you up in one place and deposits you in another without complete resolution. But whatever type of show it is, YOU MUST KNOW THE TYPE AND WORLD OF THE SHOW.

By knowing the world of the show you'll best know how *you* fit into it.

In coaching actors for Series Regular auditions, the two most common things I've found to be missing are *True Self* and *Confidence*.

1. YOUR TRUE SELF

 You need to bring all *your uniqueness*, sized appropriately, to the role.

If you've never done it in any other audition, the Series Regular is the time to bring the *real you*. Yes, you need to honor the story, need to solve the crime, cure the disease, be victorious over the bad guys, but you need to do it in your own way. If you're naturally sarcastic, bring it to the audition material. If you are naturally sweet and hopelessly optimistic, bring that quality even if you're reading for the head of a deadly organization of assassins. For maybe that spark of optimism might allow the audience to view this character as much more than a cold-hearted killer who will stop at nothing to achieve his agenda. Maybe it will show us a person who does what he does because he believes it will genuinely make the world a better place.

That is where "sized appropriately" comes into play. You want to put yourself into the role the writers have created much as you put on a piece of clothing. You want your uniqueness and personality to work *with* the world of the show, not *eclipse* it. Whatever your personal take is on life, you still need to get the job done.

2. CONFIDENCE

Possessing that spark of inner confidence that says no matter what happens, you (as the character) will rise again each week to fight another day. The Pilot introduces the audience to the Series Regulars, their world and the type of stories each episode will explore. In reading for a Series Regular role, you need to convince the powers-that-be that no matter what you're given to do each week you'll survive it; not only will you survive the challenges each episode throws at you, you'll be stronger each week because of them. An inner confidence that says "I may not win every battle, but I'll be here for every fight," tells everyone in the room you have what they need to help carry a show week after week.

You won't get every Series Regular role you ever read for. That's not bad. If you are truly bringing yourself to every Series Regular audition, it's going to be a crap shoot whether your unique way of navigating the world of the show fits the majority of opinions that will make the final decision. But by bringing yourself and all your uniqueness to the audition you will be showing them something they have not seen before, showing them something fresh. It's just a matter of time before that *something* fits perfectly.

THE PILOT SCRIPT

The Pilot is the first episode of a new series. It is the episode that sets up the world and the players. Unless it is a pilot written for a particular actor or actors, the character descriptions will be relatively general. And that is done for good reasons. The descriptions will encompass basic character traits necessary to fit in the particular world of the series and create a host of potential conflicts with this world and the other characters inhabiting it. By listing these traits, the creators are presenting the actors with some baggage, both good and bad, of the character. It is up to each actor to bring their own individual "baggage" or way of dealing with this baggage.

Here are some typical character descriptions for pilots.

BARTON 20s, a nice guy, albeit kinda lazy, maybe a little more sensitive than he'd ever want anyone to know. Barton gets dumped by Jill, his longtime girlfriend because he can't commit to a future beyond the next beer-guzzling, game-watching weekend. He'll never admit he really misses her; at least not yet, and especially since he's going to have to see her every day at work. In a fit of "I'll show you," Barton quits his job at the insurance company (owned by Jill's father) and joins his friend, LARRY, in his new one-room-in-a-lousy-part-of-town detective agency. Barton's not a detective, can't even find clean socks in the morning. But he needs a job and he figures it can't be hard to find some little old lady's cat every now and then. SERIES REGULAR

PAULA around 25, a beautiful and confident woman, from a well-to-do family. Graduated from Harvard, due in part to good grades but also to her father's generous contribution to the school, she's poised to reluctantly take a job in her father's company. But salvation arrives when she's offered a job with the NSD. What better way to show her overbearing father that she is not going to let him dictate her entire life than to take a job with an unheard of and completely under the radar (and possibly illegal for any number of reasons) intelligence agency of the U.S. government? SERIES REGULAR

Notice how not much is said about who these characters are?

BARTON - *a nice guy, maybe a little more sensitive than he'd ever want anyone to know.*

That's about as general as you can get. The rest of the information is *what happens* to Barton to get him to the place where the pilot begins. The same is true for the role of Paula.

PAULA - *around 25, a beautiful and confident woman, from a well-to-do family.*

Even less than what is said about Barton. Much more time in both descriptions is given to these characters' stories, telling us what has happened and what is going to happen to them.

Let's take a couple more descriptions.

JOHN RAMOS - In his early 30s, John is a wreck; he hasn't shaved in a week or changed his clothes. He is on the verge of a psychotic break. His whole life he has been abused, starting with his mother trading him for a bottle of whiskey, to being repeatedly abused by his foster parents. He joined the army to escape the foster system but was dishonorably discharged over an ugly episode in Iraq where fifteen civilians were mowed down; a crime his commanding officer committed but blamed on John. When John saves a drowning child, for the first time in his life he's heralded as something other than an outcast. Maybe, just maybe, with the help of the local sheriff, Alice, he might be able to turn his life around; that is until his old commanding officer surfaces with an agenda that, this time, is more deadly than a dishonorable discharge. SERIES REGULAR

This one gives a lot more information about "who" John is. More than just physical attributes, the bit of story included serves to uncover the pain and suffering that has gone into making John the man he is today. This story also serves to hint at the difficult journeys that lie ahead for John.

I have to say that these descriptions are not from the pilot script. They are typical of what would be released through something like Breakdown Services®. If you don't receive this description when you get the audition, ask for it, either from your representation or from the casting office. These descriptions were written by someone who read the entire script and summarized it to give you a picture of the character. The actual character descriptions in the script will be even sparser.

HOW THE SERIES REGULAR AUDITION WORKS

Your initial audition or auditions will most probably consist of reading with the Casting Director and/or their assistant. During this audition they are looking at you to see if you not only fit the broader parameters of the character but, if not, to see if you might be right for another role in the series. They are getting a sense of who you are and what you can bring to the show. You may or may not get adjustments. [2]

THE CHEMISTRY READ

If you're right for the role you will eventually be brought in for a Chemistry Read. This is where you are paired with other potential Series Regulars to see what kind of chemistry you have together. If your character has a significant other in the show, you'll be brought together with other actors reading for that character to see how you interact.

DO NOT TRY TO SECOND GUESS WHAT THEY WANT TO SEE WITH REGARD TO CHEMISTRY.

Let the chemistry be what it is. Many actors have lost parts because they decided they needed to be all lovey dovey with the actor reading for their love-interest, or deeply antagonistic with an actor reading for their character's enemy. If you've done your homework and know who you are and who the other character is and what they represent to you, your natural chemistry with the other actor will be enough. You may get the part because of the mildly combative relationship that is naturally there between you and your love interest. You may get the part because you don't come across as one-sided in dealing with your enemy, but because you have a sense of compassion for them that will make the stories all that more interesting when you have to butt heads. If the chemistry doesn't work this time, it will work another time. The freer you are with who you are, what you are and how you are, the easier it will be for everyone involved to see how you can fit into their show. And if not this show, then another one. Remember, just as this won't be your last audition, it probably isn't the last show the Casting Director and Producers will do. I've gotten many roles

---

[2] An adjustment is a direction given to an actor during an audition.

from people who didn't use me in one project but brought me in for another at a later time.

READING FOR A SERIES LEAD

There are a couple types of Series Regulars. The Series *Leads* are exactly as described, the leads of the show. The show revolves around them and they are central to the story each week. They are the characters the audiences will tune in to follow. Most often in reading for a Series Regular Lead your first audition will begin with one or more scenes. You may not get an entire script at first so you will have to base your work on the scenes you're given. These scenes will be given to you to see not only what you bring to the character initially but also to see how you negotiate the arc of the story.

PREP WORK FOR A SERIES REGULAR LEAD

When you dissect your scene(s) for a Series Regular Lead audition, you have to add another layer to your prep work. A Pilot is not meant to be a stand-alone story. Though it could stand alone, it is meant to introduce a world and its inhabitants. As such, it is imperative when reading scenes in a pilot to extract any and all information that clues you into what might happen throughout an entire season.

Let me give you an example. Take a standard police procedural or cop show. Pretty much guaranteed that one of the WHERES is going to be a precinct or police station. An actor prepping a scene might write, "WHERE – the precinct where I work, my desk." Accurate. But let's look at this WHERE from a larger viewpoint. Let's call it the SERIES WHERE: "The main precinct in a major U.S. city, where the cops are more than just co-workers; they look at each other as family. A place where the main characters come together to do a job they love." Do you see how that has so much more power than merely "the precinct where I work, my desk?" By understanding that this *Where* is a place the audience will come to every week, a place with a particular tone, it gives it more importance and will affect the actor more deeply than a mere work-place *Where* would. It sets up this precinct as a safe place, a place of "family," but one that will probably include drama. If the cops look at each other as family, what family doesn't have drama? And drama at "home" can be very difficult. The feel of this precinct would be very different from one where everyone hated the captain, where all the detectives were trying to outdo each other, where smiles were all false and friendships even more false. That *Where* would have a whole different feel to it.

By looking at the scene or scenes from the larger Series perspective you can more fully understand the particular challenges and journeys of the scene or scenes. Is the journey in a scene one that will be completed by the end of the show, such as catching the bad guys, or is it a journey that will carry on throughout one or possibly many more seasons? If a character has trouble trusting himself and his instincts, is this something he will be able to do by the end of the pilot or is it something he will deal with the entire season or seasons to come? If it is a recurring challenge it will be a much more subtle journey than one that is resolved by the end of the pilot.

Not every Prep entry will have an obvious expansive Series layer to it. The WHERE will most probably have a Series layer to it, especially if it is a place we will return to time after time. The WHO will as well, but be careful not to dissect and plan too much on the WHO. Realize that WHO you are is a character who will grow and change over the course of the series, sometimes quickly and quite a lot, sometimes very slowly and in small increments. It will depend on the show's Writers and Producers as well as your own uniqueness and instincts. Just be aware that you are at the beginning of a journey and as such you must be open to growth and change.

Here are two scenes from a pilot script. I gave these scenes to four actors. Two were reading the part of Barton, the Series Regular Lead, and two were reading for Jill. I will discuss the Jill auditions in the next chapter on Series Regular Supporting Characters.

For the actors reading Barton, I had them bring in their individual Prep work for each scene. In class we did the Series Prep work together, after which they read the scenes.

SIDE ONE

ACT ONE

FADE IN:

EXT – BEACH – DAY – SANTA MONICA, CALIFORNIA

The sun glistens off the sparkling blue water as tanned beauties, men and women, cavort along the sands wearing little more than minute pieces of fabric on their perfect bodies. The camera pans up, catching a red Ferrari as it zooms along Pacific Coast Highway.

INT. APARTMENT – SANTA MONICA – SAME

A man's hand unlatches an old wooden frame window. The hand bangs and bangs, but the window only opens about two inches. Noise and a wisp of air seep through the small opening, bouncing off the cracked brick wall of another building that sits a few feet away across a litter-strewn walkway. This is the wondrous view from this *beach pad*.

The camera pans back to reveal BARTON JO-
HANSSEN, 28, in a torn tank top and
Christmas Plaid boxers. He shuffles
through a pile of dirty clothes and makes
his way to the bathroom. He passes an
open closet, not noticing that half of
the rack is empty.

> BARTON
> Jill you make coffee?

Barton shuffles out of the bedroom and
into the…

INT. LIVING ROOM - SAME

The miniscule living room is overpowered
by a huge flat screen television. Barton
hears a noise from the kitchen and turns
to see JILL HATHAWAY, 27, walking out of
the kitchen, a sack of groceries in her
hand. A bag of potato chips pokes out
from the top of the sack. She pauses for
a second when she sees Barton, then walks
to the front door. Two suitcases sit next
to the front door.

> BARTON
> Where are you going
> with the potato chips?

> JILL
> I'm only taking enough
> food fora couple of
> days.

                    BARTON
          Yeah, but that's the
          last bag of mustard
          bar-b-que chips.
          They're super hard to
          find.

                    JILL
          Barton! Stop it. I'm
          leaving you.

                    BARTON
          You... what?

                    JILL
          I'm sorry... I...

                    BARTON
          No... it's ok. You can
          have the chips.

                    JILL
          It's not about the
          chips!

Barton notices the suitcases for the
first time.

                    BARTON
          What's going on? I
          don't understand.

                    JILL
          Look around you. What
          do you see?

                    BARTON
Our apartment. Where
we live together.

                    JILL
I see a shitty little
hole in the wall.

                    BARTON
Well a beach apartment
is expensive.

                    JILL
We don't have a beach
apartment! Look out
the window, do you see
the water?

                    BARTON
No, because...

                    JILL
Because it's not
there. Yes there is an
ocean somewhere past
the falling down ware-
house next door, but
we're nowhere near it.
But that's not the
worst part. Do you
know what today is?

                    BARTON
What? Oh God, I'm so
sorry, happy birthday
honey!

                    JILL
It's not my birthday.
I moved in here a year
ago today. Do you re-
member what you said
to me the day I moved
in?

                    BARTON
Ah... I'm glad you're
here?

                    JILL
You told me six months
tops, we'd be out of
here. We agreed to
save money each month
to get an apartment
with at least the
smell of the ocean if
not an actual view of
it. Each month *I've*
put money aside but
you haven't.

                    BARTON
 I've tried! It's just
that....

                    JILL
          I don't want to hear
          any more "it's just
          that." I've been hear-
          ing them for six
          months! Six months of
          tripping over your
          dirty underwear on the
          floor, your beer cans
          in the trash…your….

                    BARTON
          I'm sorry about the
          mess. The guys… after
          the game, it was so
          late… I didn't want to
          wake you cleaning up.

Jill starts to cry.

                    JILL (Cont'd)
          I promised myself I
          wouldn't cry!

                    BARTON
          Honey…

Barton reaches for her. She backs away.

                    JILL
          No. I won't let you do
          this to me.

                    BARTON
          Do what?

                    JILL
          Touch me because...
          every time you hold me
          I... just stay here.

                    BARTON
          I'm sorry.

Barton looks at her with his lost, ador-
able puppy look.

                    JILL
          Don't do that either!
          Don't give me that
          "helpless little boy"
          look.

                    BARTON
          I'm not doing...

                    JILL
          Barton, you need to
          grow up. I love you,
          but I can't do this
          anymore.

Jill turns towards the door.

                    BARTON
          But I thought we were
          going to get married?

                    JILL
          So did I. But I want
          to marry a man, not a
          child.

Jill gives Barton a quick kiss on the cheek.

                    JILL
          Don't be late for
          work. You know how
          daddy hates it.

Jill walks to the front door and opens it.

                    BARTON
          Where are you going
          to...

CARLOTTA MENDEZ, 26, stands there. Her 6 foot 1 inch shimmering beauty is scarred by the look of sheer contempt on her face as she takes in Barton and the mess in the apartment.

                    JILL
          I'm moving in with
          Carlotta until I can
          get my own place.

Jill grabs one of the suitcases and walks out of the apartment. Carlotta walks in, looking down at John as she picks up the other suitcase.

                    CARLOTTA
          What a pig.

Carlotta walks out of the apartment, slamming the door behind her. Barton looks around, not sure what to do next.

SIDE TWO

INT. LARRY PERKINS DETECTIVE AGENCY -
LATER

LARRY PERKINS, 30, leans back in his
chair behind his desk. Or rather, a door
on two saw horses that passes for his
desk. The window behind him is as grimy
as the neighborhood, and it's a good
thing it's dirty as the view isn't much.
Barton is pacing, weaving his way through
the boxes that clutter the small office.

> BARTON
> I can't believe she
> just dumped me!

> LARRY
> Dude, really? You
> didn't see this com-
> ing?

> BARTON
> No! Did you?

> LARRY
> You live like a col-
> lege kid! In a pit
> with a fridge full of
> beer and occasionally
> some limp lettuce.

> BARTON
> We don't eat at home
> very much.

                    LARRY
That's because there's
never anything to eat.
Believe me, I know.
I've trie

to raid your fridge
plenty of times.

                    BARTON
But I thought we were
happy.

                    LARRY
You were happy. You
had free sex all week
and watched football
all week-end with your
buds. Women want a tad
bit more than that.

                    BARTON
Oh, so you're the ex-
pert on women? How
many times you been
married?

                    LARRY
Two and a half. One
was a Vegas weekend…
that doesn't count as
a whole. But, yes, I'm
an expert compared to
you. Women want a
home, a place to nest,
to be cozy and have
kids.

                    BARTON
Kids? No, no, no, we
discussed that. Jill
has a career.

                    LARRY
She has a career be-
cause her dad owns the
company. But if the
option of grandkids
comes along, old
daddy'll uproot her
career path in a
heartbeat. And, uh
speaking of career
paths, you do know
yours is down the toi-
let with this latest
turn of events.

                    BARTON
Way ahead of you… I
quit. I'm not going to
give her dad the sat-
isfaction of dumping
me too.

LARRY

Well, look at you, getting pro active all of a sudden. Maybe there is hope for you after all. So what are you going to do now?

BARTON

I have no idea.

LARRY

I do. Why don't you come and work with me?

BARTON

Where? Here?

LARRY

Sure. Why not?

BARTON

I… I don't know anything about being a Private Eye.

LARRY

What else you gonna do? You got another job lined up?

BARTON

No. I didn't really plan on all this happening.

LARRY
Life hands you a doo-
doo you make a mud
pie.

BARTON
That doesn't make any
sense.

LARRY
Whatever, the point is
you gotta do some
thing. Especially if
you want to keep your
beach pad.

BARTON
Beach pad? You just
said it was a pit.

LARRY
It is. But it's your
pit. And I'd hate to
see you lose it. So
what do you say? Just
give it a try. I'm
your best friend. You
and me working to-
gether, how bad could
it be? Actually don't
answer that. Answer
this instead: you ever
thought what it'd be
like to get up every
day and go to work to
actually *help* people?

                    BARTON
No… and neither did
you.

                    LARRY
Precisely my point.
You know me, we're the
same. We'd be a terri-
fic team, unbeatable.
I'll teach you every-
thing you need to
know.

                    BATON
Where'd you learn how
to be a detective?

                    LARRY
Correspondence course.
I got the CD's right
here, you can start
listening to them
right now. By this af-
ternoon, you'll be a
pro.

                    BARTON
Larry, I don't know.

                    LARRY
Look, I'll level with
you. I don't know ei-
ther. But ever since I
was a kid I wanted to
be a detective. Just
felt right. So last
year I bought this
course, and here I am.
Larry Perkins, Private
Dick. And having you,
my best friend, work
with me… that feels
right too.

                    BARTON
Do you make enough
money to pay two sala-
ries?

                    LARRY
Not yet… but we will.
I got a really good
feeling about this.
What do you say?

                    BARTON
It's not like anything
else is knocking at my
door. What the Hell.
But I need to make
some money. Soon.

> LARRY
>
> Money's no problem. We
> get a bunch of clients
> we'll be on easy
> street.

> BARTON
>
> And if we don't get a
> bunch of clients?

> LARRY
>
> We'll be *on* the real
> street. But, hey,
> we'll be together!

Larry is beaming as he leans back in his chair even more. Suddenly, BAM, he goes crashing backwards. Larry raises his arms.

> LARRY
>
> I'm fine, fine.

Barton puts his head in his hands. What has he gotten himself into?

The two actors I had read for Barton are almost complete opposites. Glenn is tall with classically chiseled features, a typical "Hollywood" leading man. The second actor, Ashton, is average height with very curly hair. He is attractive, just not in a typical leading man way. He is much more of a "character" actor.

Let's discuss Glenn's audition first.

KEVIN: Tell me your prep work for both scenes

GLENN: For the first scene:

WHERE – In my apartment that I share with Jill, my girlfriend.

WHEN – Morning, after I just got up.

WHAT – My girlfriend tells me she's leaving me.
WHY – I don't understand why she's leaving me.
WHO – I'm a guy who's being dumped by my girlfriend.
STORY WHY – To set up *who* I am.

For the second scene:
WHERE – In Larry's office.
WHEN – After I've been dumped by Jill and quit my job.
WHAT – Larry asks me to work with him.
WHY – I need a job and Larry offers me one.
WHO – I'm a guy without a job and no other offers.
STORY WHY – To get me into the Private Eye business.

KEVIN: All right let's do the Series Prep together. As I said earlier, when reading for a Series Regular Lead in a pilot, you have to do another level of prep work. This comes with a word of caution because the last thing I want you to do is to over-analyze the material. But when reading for a Series Regular Lead it's not enough to simply look at the scene or scenes you're going to read in the audition. Understand that a pilot is a story that sets up the entire series. As such, it is not only introducing the audience to the world of the show and the inhabitants of this world, it is introducing the paths the characters will take. It introduces their strengths, their weaknesses and, most importantly, the challenges the characters will face, at least for the first season. So in your Series Prep Work you need to look at *how your character is being set up* for the challenges and growth he or she will experience through the *entire season*, and not just the pilot episode.

GLENN: But how do you do that if you don't have any other scripts? How can you do prep for a story you don't know?

KEVIN: By reading the script you *do* have and looking at it as a starting point, a place from which many more stories will grow and by expanding your vision of the scenes.

Let's take your prep work first. WHERE – in your apartment with Jill, your girlfriend. That's correct from the perspective of this scene and this single script. But for our Series Prep we're going to add another layer of prep. What does the scene say about the apartment?

GLENN: It says it's an old place with a view of a brick wall. It's messy, clothes everywhere, and small.

KEVIN: Exactly. But it also tells us who Barton is. He is like his apartment, a mess, unfocused. So a SERIES WHERE might read "in Barton's apartment that, until this morning, was everything he wanted and needed. But it is about to change and it will no longer be the safe and snug little world he thought it was."

Now let's take your WHEN. You said "the morning after I just got up." Take that and expand it.

SERIES WHEN – "A day that probably begins like many other days, but a day that is about to uproot his whole life and change his world."

For your WHAT you said "my girlfriend tells me she's leaving me."

SERIES WHAT could be "Jill, my fiancée, leaves me because I haven't lived up to the promise I made her to change. Her leaving me is the beginning of my life being turned upside down. She tells me I behave like a child and challenges me to act like a man instead."

Everything here is written clearly in this first scene but with this SERIES WHAT it takes you beyond the first scene and sets up the idea that Barton will most likely struggle with responsibility and maturity throughout the entire season. At least as far as Jill is concerned.

Your scene WHY was "I don't understand why she's leaving me."

SERIES WHY – "I have been totally clueless that Jill was unhappy with me and the way I live. What else have I been clueless about? I didn't live up to my promise to save money for a better place, I have been living in my own little world not seeing that my tunnel vision has pushed my fiancée to leave me and brought my whole world crashing down. Her leaving me just might force me to at least recognize my faults and maybe do something about fixing them. My life will never be the same."

For your WHO in the first scene, you wrote "I'm a guy who's being dumped by my girlfriend." That's a little light, don't you think?

GLENN: I guess. But I thought we were supposed to keep it to one sentence.

KEVIN: That's a guideline to help you consolidate everything into a clear and easily understandable idea. But the sentence needs to include all pertinent facts. You totally ignored the fact that you broke a promise to save money to move, are too lazy to clean up after yourself and your friends, make excuses as to why you didn't clean up and, according to your fiancée, are more like a child than a man; a man who works at a company owned by his fiancée's father. All pretty important information about Barton. Can you put all that in one sentence? Sure you can. Try.

GLENN: Ok. Let's see… I'm a guy, a lazy guy who would rather party with his buds than honor a promise I made to my fiancée to move to a better place, a guy who works at my fiancée's dad's company, a guy who makes excuses for his actions, I'm more like a boy than a man.

KEVIN: Much better. Yeah, it's a long sentence, but this a Series Regular Lead. There has to be a lot to him or there'd be no show. Now, want to try a Series Who for Barton?

GLENN: Sure. Barton is a man who has his life turned upside down when his fiancée walks out on him. He's a guy who will have to grow up if he wants to get his life in order.

KEVIN: Very good. This isn't to say that the entire series will only be about Barton "growing up." But Barton's becoming more and more responsible will most assuredly be a recurring theme. And Barton's accepting the challenge to become more than he is in the beginning gives you a character with much more depth than one who is merely "a guy who is dumped by his fiancée." And if you're reading for a Series Lead, you better deliver some depth.

Ashton, you're also reading for Barton. I'm not going to ask you about your prep work yet, but I'd like you to also take some time to look over your work and add to it the Series Prep Work we just discussed.

I gave Glenn and Ashton a bit of time to go over their personal Prep Work as well as the added Series Prep Work. Glenn read first. He was very animated, really hitting the twists of the scene very hard.

KEVIN: How did that go for you?

GLENN: I didn't like what I did at all.

KEVIN: Why?

GLENN: It felt like, I don't know, like I was really pushing it.

KEVIN: You were. You were way over the top, trying much too hard. I've never seen you do that before.

GLENN: Yeah, but I… this was the lead so I wanted to really make an impression.

KEVIN: Unfortunately the impression was over the top. You hit us over the head. You're reading for a Series Regular Lead. Your character will be in most, if not every scene of the pilot. We will get an entire show to learn who you are. But you decided since you only had two scenes to show us who you are, you had to throw everything you had at us. You had so much going on that it was hard to watch you in these *two* scenes. Can you imagine an audience trying to sit through an entire show of that?

GLENN: Yes, but I wanted to really get into the stuff I felt going on with Barton. I felt that… I don't know, that I needed to show you that I understood who Barton is and what is going on with him. That he's really a guy who has had his whole life turned upside down.

KEVIN: Yes he is, but you were so concerned with making sure we knew that *you* knew the entire scope and all the dire ramifications of these two scenes that you forgot that these two scenes, though contributions to the whole story, are merely *part* of the whole story. You can't act the whole show in two scenes. The people auditioning you know the show, they know how the scenes you're given to use for the audition fit in to the story. But in order for the story and you in the story to work, you can't go beyond what happens in these scenes and play the end. You went through that first scene incredibly hyped up. Barton doesn't know that his whole world is about to change forever; at least not *yet*. Until Jill walks out the door at the end of the scene she is still there and his world is relatively unchanged. And even after she walks out at the end of the scene, how do you know she's not coming back the next scene? The actor knows it but Barton doesn't. So while you have to have an awareness, maybe a deep-seated fear that your life *could* be about to drastically change, until you're given a scene where you know for sure that it *has changed*, you can't overtly play that. And the worst part of all is that you totally denied who *you* are, totally buried your own uniqueness in your efforts to show me that you knew Barton is a man on the edge of a life-changing abyss.

GLENN: What do you mean?

KEVIN: Glenn, you're a very attractive man; but not only in looks. You have a subtleness to your personality that draws people to you, that "attracts" them. You don't generally have big reactions, you're not hyperactive, you don't often jump up and down, speak loudly or use your hands to emphasize a point. You're pretty laid-back. But your eyes are extremely expressive. When you're just being yourself, you don't need to move much for me to know what's going on with you. We've had discussions and critiques where I've seen you affected very deeply. Something in your eyes and subtle changes in your face reflect it, these speak volumes.

Remember, this is an on-camera show. I don't need to go into discussing the size of the performance being too big for the camera because I know you already know it was too big. But it's not just about the size of your performance. It's about you allowing who you naturally are work *for* you, not *against* you. If you approach Barton as man who is *you*, a man who doesn't show his feelings with overt gestures but with his eyes, you are giving an audition that is *unique to you*. By overplaying physically, talking loudly with a frantic, almost desperate energy, you directed my attention *away* from your eyes, away from your strength, away from who you are. So I saw a man *acting* desperate instead of *feeling* desperate. And that is not you.

Reading for a Series Regular Lead *requires* that you know who you are and how you come across, especially on camera. Everyone is made up of many, many facets, but we don't show them all the time or all at once. In your audition it seemed as if you tried to do that, tried to show me every facet you possess instead of trusting that the select few facets you use in everyday life would be enough. And they are. If you understand who Barton is and what is happening to him, and ingest it, allow it to become part of you and allow yourself to express what is happening to Barton as you would if it happened to you, it will be enough. More than enough, it will be exactly right: *for you*.

As I said before, a Series Regular Lead is a character whose journey will take place, hopefully, over a long period of time. It is someone who needs to reach out and touch the audience in such a way to make them return, week after week, to be with you. The producers are looking for someone people will want in their home, someone they will want to follow like an entire ocean of "peeping Toms." To give a successful Series Regular Lead audition, you need to be unafraid to see the character's world through your own eyes and to throw yourself into that world with your own, individual way of being without eclipsing or denying the story. By doing that you will give an audition that will be personal; yours.

ASHTON'S AUDITION

KEVIN: Ashton, I read your prep work and it is pretty close to Glenn's so there is no need to really discuss it unless there is something you don't understand or want to discuss further.

ASHTON: No, it was pretty clear. I see the difference in doing just the scene's prep work and adding the Series prep work.

KEVIN: Good, then let's get to your audition. Funny, you did the exact opposite of Glenn. Whereas Glenn gave us too much, you didn't give us enough.

ASHTON: I gotta say something. I… I mean I felt strange reading for this role. I'm nothing like Glenn. He's Hollywood handsome and I'm not. I feel like a nerd next to him. There's no way I'd get an audition for a part like this.

KEVIN: I'm going to stop you right there. Nothing could be further from the truth, for many reasons. First of all, what's your definition of a nerd?

ASHTON: I don't know… weird, geeky character guy I guess.

KEVIN: I can think of a number of adjectives to describe you but weird and geeky aren't two of them. *Charactery*, yes; by that I mean that your personality is an integral part of your looks. When someone is classically handsome or beautiful it is their looks that we generally notice first. Their personality is there as well but it usually isn't as overtly dominant a feature as their looks. I'm not saying their personalities aren't important, not at all. I'm saying that very attractive people who are comfortable with their looks know that because of their looks most people will give them positive attention, at least at first. The well-rounded ones know that looks will only go so far in *keeping* someone's attention and they have personalities as well. But for what I like to call *charactery* people, their personalities are right up front along with their looks. They present both immediately, at the same time. It is a combination of personality and looks that draw people to them, not looks or personality alone.

But you seem to be convinced that Barton is supposed to be a classically handsome man. Where in the script or in the character breakdown does it say anything about Barton being an Adonis?

ASHTON: Nowhere, but if I walked into an audition room and I saw Glenn reading for the same part, it'd be pretty obvious to me what they wanted.

KEVIN: I love how you immediately jump to the conclusion that he's what they want instead of you being what they want and Glenn being the exception. Right away you've sabotaged your audition by deciding Glenn, even a room full of Glenns is what the producers want. If that were the case, why were you called in?

ASHTON: I don't know.

KEVIN: I'll tell you why you would be called in and why I gave you this audition piece. In auditioning a pilot, no one really knows what they want or which way they definitely want to go until they see the actors. They know the story, have an *idea* which way they want to go, but any pre-conceived notions they have are based on what they have experienced so far. Let me give you what may seem a bizarre example. You're from Ohio, aren't you?

ASHTON: Yes.

KEVIN: Do you like sushi?

ASHTON: What? Yeah, love it.

KEVIN: Had you ever eaten it growing up?

ASHTON: Never.

KEVIN: So until you first tried it, if anyone asked you what food you absolutely loved, you never would have said sushi.

ASHTON: No way. I only tried on a dare. But I'm glad I did.

KEVIN: It's exactly the same with casting, particularly a pilot. The Producers read the script and form various opinions on how to fill the roles. But these opinions are invariably based on what the people involved already know. Maybe they have certain actors in mind and if those actors aren't available, they've called in other actors who are similar. But a good Casting Director knows countless actors, far more than most producers. And part of the Casting Director's job is to give the Producers choices, give them ways other than the obvious ones to fill roles. Many a major casting decision has been made that was a direct opposite to what the Producers originally had in mind. And until they saw the actor who was the opposite, they would have never imagined him or her in the role. But once they saw them audition, much like you with sushi, they were hooked. Did you know that the series Harry's Law, starring Kathy Bates as Harry, was originally written for a man? Yet sometime during the pre-production process someone came up with the brilliant idea to make Harry a woman, and voila, Kathy Bates. And she is not only wonderful in the part, the whole show took on a new meaning and feel with her in the part as opposed to a man.

But putting that aside, as I pointed out before there is nothing in the script that indicates Barton's looks. Yes, it's Television and yes, in Television nearly all of the time they cast attractive people as Series Leads, but Ashton, there is nothing unattractive about you. You are quirky, definitely more *charactery* than Glenn, but I don't think anyone would look at you and immediately decide you'd only be right for a three-week-old-dead zombie.

ASHTON: (laughing) That'd be fun.

KEVIN: It probably would be. But just as Glenn has his appealing attributes, so do you. Whereas Glenn is quiet and his eyes are intense you have of a kind of offbeat, eager innocence to you. For example when I've described something in class that is a new concept to everyone, Glenn looks at me directly while he processes the information while you tend to look away and talk to yourself, repeating what I said as if speaking the words helps you understand it. You have your own way of looking at and dealing with the world and though it is different than Glenn's, it is not only valid being yours, it is charming in itself. I can definitely see you playing Barton. It would be different than Glenn's Barton, but no less appealing and successful. But in your audition you seemed to be trying to be like Glenn. You were very reserved, very contained, letting none of your personality into the audition.

There is no way you are going to be Glenn, so don't try. If you walk into a room full of Glenns, so what? It's even more important to be true to yourself and show them Ashton's version of Barton. No matter who you are, looks alone aren't enough to carry a Series Lead role; it also takes personality. You took all your personality out of your audition and made your audition not a particularly memorable one. You said all the words but the most I can say is that you didn't get in the way of the story; you certainly didn't enhance it.

I can't stress this enough in every audition, but especially when reading for a Series Lead. Everyone auditioning for the role is going to be reading the same words, acting in the same set of circumstances, putting themselves in the same world of the show. If you don't bring your unique being into the read as well, you're showing the Producers nothing but a mere vocalization of the script. I'm not saying to thrust your personality into the audition to *eclipse* the script, but do allow your personality to be present and available so that it *enhances* the script.

GLENN: In other words, just be real.

KEVIN: I'll answer that with a modified yes, and a big NO. I know a common catch phrase among acting workshops is the "just be real" mantra, but as we've discussed in our regular classes, ACTING IS NOT REAL LIFE. The things that happen in a story, in real life, would happen over the course of hours, days, weeks, months, years, sometimes decades. But everything in our story, in one episode, will actually happen in an hour at most. So it's not "real life" as much as it is LIFE CONDENSED.

This is an important distinction. You have to be real in that you have to put your real self in the audition, but you have to do it with an acute awareness of all that has happened, is happening, and all that might happen in the future, without giving too much away. It's a tricky dance, especially for a Series Regular Lead.

The job of the Series Regular Lead is to take all the information given and piece it together to reach some sort of conclusion. Whether it's the right conclusion, the wrong conclusion or merely a conclusion that produces more questions than answers depends upon the show. But if an audience is going to want to tune in each episode, the Series Regular Lead has to be someone who not only leads them on the journey or treasure hunt, but someone who silently encourages the audience's participation in the journey. The audience not only watches a show, they want to solve the problems right along with you. By doing too much you take that away from them by hitting the audience over the head with what is happening and what your character's take on it is. By not doing enough, you rob the audience of any sense of importance to anything that is happening and they will quickly lose interest. But by doing just enough in your own, unique way, you bring the audience along with you on the journey and you bring them along in a way no one else can. Your challenge each week will be to give the story, and through it the audience, just enough of yourself to make them want to go on each week's journey with you. And they will go on this journey not only to see how each week's challenge is resolved, but to see how you have changed and grown with the resolution.

No matter who you are, no matter if you're handsome, quirky, beautiful, zany, you have to know who you are and bring who you are to every audition. If you're totally wrong for the role, you're totally wrong for the role. By throwing yourself one hundred percent into the audition, you will show everyone what roles you are totally *right* for.

CHAPTER 10

THE EPISODIC SERIES REGULAR SECONDARY CHARACTER AUDITION

I had two actresses, Laura and Ashley, read for Jill. Laura, a brunette in her thirties, has a sophisticated air about her, a very east coast vibe Ashley is blond, twenties, and is much more Southern California laid back.

KEVIN: I'm going to discuss both of your auditions together. But to start, let's have both of you tell me your prep work.

LAURA: WHERE – The apartment I shared with my boyfriend for a year, until today.

WHEN – Morning, the day I decided to leave Barton.

WHAT – Because he can't figure it out, I have to explain to Barton why I'm leaving him.

WHY – He is so self-centered, so clueless, I have to spell it out for him.

WHO – I'm a woman who can't wait anymore for her boyfriend to grow up.

STORY WHY – To get me out of Barton's life.

KEVIN: Ok, Ashley, tell me yours.

ASHLEY: WHERE – The dumpy apartment where I live, or lived, with my fiancé.

WHEN – When I'm fed up with him and I'm moving out.

WHAT – I'm telling Barton I can't live with him anymore, can't live like this.

WHY – He's never going to change so I have to leave.

WHO – I'm an angry and hurt woman who has to admit she's made a big mistake.

STORY WHY – To start the dominoes in Barton's life falling.

KEVIN: I love that Story Why! I'm going to discuss both your auditions together because they were pretty much identical. You both gave your own uniqueness but both your auditions had a similar tone. Now that you've both told me your prep work, I can see why. Both of you latched onto Jill's anger and resentment very well; too well. Laura, you were stern, unforgiving and determined to let Barton know that you weren't going to take his crap anymore. Ashley, you were in "full bitch" mode. I don't mean to imply that you weren't justified in that. It's clear from the sides that Barton is nowhere near being the man you need him to be, despite his promise to be that man. This scene is a direct result of Barton's failings. Both of you recognized that and both of you spelled it out for him very clearly. It's his fault you're leaving. But this scene is about much more than that. Especially since Jill is going to be a Series Regular or at the very least a recurring character.

Barton is the lead of this series. He's the character around whom the stories will revolve, the main person the audience will tune in to see each episode. Despite his multitude of failings, the audience needs to like him since he is the main reason they're going to tune in each week. The audience is going to be super-sensitive to anyone who causes him discord. Pointing out his flaws is fine. Giving him a hard time about them is fine. Pushing him to change and grow is great. But if *all* you do is *attack* him, even though what you say may be true, the audience isn't going to like you. I'm not saying the audience has to like every character all the time. But they need to see you have a positive connection with Barton, at least *some* of the time. Jill is Barton's love interest, at least for now. And that love is very clearly written in this scene. But both of you chose to ignore it, or gloss over it.

LAURA: But she's leaving him for very strong and specific reasons, because he failed her, failed to do what he promised.

KEVIN: Yes, that's true. But it's also true that she cares about him so much that if he touches her she won't go. If he gives her that "little boy" face, the very face that probably caused her to fall in love with him, she may not go. And when she does go, does she curse him and slam the door? No, she kisses him and urges him not to be late for work because her father, his boss, won't like it. So even though she's leaving him, she is concerned about him and his welfare. Both of you fell into the trap of only showing Jill's anger and frustration with Barton and not any of her love for him. I could understand that if that was all that was written. But it's not. And even if that was all that was written, I'd still have a problem with it.

Jill is not only just Barton's ex, she is one of the two people in the story who know him best. Larry, his best friend, is the other one. By only playing Jill's anger, you limit the possibilities of your relationship with Barton. You set yourself up as his enemy, no matter how justified you are. But if you also explore and give us an inkling of the love you not only *had* for Barton, but *still have*, you open up a world of possibilities.

When you read for a Series Regular you have to not only portray what's written on the paper, but you have to bring in some thing or things that pique our interest, something that makes the Producers and Writers ask themselves, "Wow, where else can this relationship go?" Jill is in a unique position to allow the audience to see Barton from a different side than any other character. She loves him, has lived with him, and is the one who first presents the challenge for him to change. Who better to gauge whether he will really change or remain the same, just in different circumstances? If you play Jill only as an angry, spurned partner, you limit the effect you can have upon Barton and the story, because the audience and more importantly the Writers and Producers, will only see you as Barton's enemy. Though you can't know just from these two scenes when and/or how Jill will reenter Barton's life, chances are she will reappear throughout the life of the series. Therefore you have to bring in something that gives the audience hope, something that doesn't make them cringe every time they see you. Since you only have one scene for this audition, it is imperative that it not be one level.

If you see something, no matter how small in Barton to love, the audience will see it also. So Jill's job is to not only turn Barton's life upside down and let the audience see how messed up he and his life is, it is also to let them know that there is hope. Someone loves him and wherever there is love, there is hope.

ASHLEY: I felt myself being just a total bitch, but I couldn't stop myself.

KEVIN: I think much of the fault lies in your prep work, specifically the way you saw Barton. Both of you wrote nothing but pretty intense negatives about him. Laura, in your WHY you wrote that Barton "is so self-centered, so clueless," and Ashley you wrote "He's never going to change." So you both set yourselves up to treat him negatively as you didn't allow anything good about Barton to become part of you. You both ignored the Writer when he wrote that you were extremely sensitive to Barton's touching you, so vulnerable that you could change your mind about leaving. You also ignored the fact that you give him a kiss at the end of the scene. Even though Jill makes a pretty big point about not wanting Barton to touch her because it might make her change her mind, she can't resist touching him, giving him a good-bye kiss. This tells me that no matter how many negatives you throw at him, there is a pretty strong positive there as well.

Watch any successful Television show, one that's been on for more than two seasons. Look at the Series Regular antagonists, the ones who've been on for more than one season. They may be antagonistic most of the time. But there will be times when they show the Series Lead or Leads some understanding, if not outright compassion. If they're merely evil combatants, the audience will tire of them after a while because they and their relationship with the Lead or Leads will have no dimension other than the same old, same old.

This is especially true when there is a chance, no matter how remote, for a loving relationship. Doesn't have to be huge and obvious, in fact it's better if it's not. But a subtle inkling, a chance that maybe it's possible there is something more than combat, will keep interests piqued and audiences watching. And that is what Producers are looking for when they cast Series Regulars; actors and actresses who can lure an audience into tuning in episode after episode. Pique their interest and you've got them hooked.

When a series is green lit, along with a pilot script, anywhere from one to three years' worth of stories have been plotted out. But the real exciting part of a new series is Casting. This is where the Producers and Writers are not only looking for actors who will fit in with the storylines they've already envisioned, but for actors and actresses who will *enhance* those stories, who will bring in qualities that will inspire the *way* those stories will play out. A way to do that is to take every bit of essential information in any and all scenes you're given and explore the *possibilities* those bits of information open up.

Remember the purpose of a pilot is to set up a story. It is a combination of back-story *exposition*, current story *exploration* and future story *evolution*. If you want to be a Series Regular in a story, your audition must have all three of those elements as well. For your audition, you have to not only look for the story that *is* presented in the scenes you're given, but for the possibilities of other stories that are *suggested* in those scenes and subtly include those possibilities in who and how you are. Unlike a Guest Star or Co-Star role, a Series Regular role doesn't end its arc in one episode. It is a role with a life and arcs that will span the entire season and, hopefully, for many seasons to come. You have to make sure you approach a Series Regular audition with a sense of an arc that expands beyond the parameters of the pilot. In doing that, in addition to showing the Producers and writers a character who is living in the scene you're given, you will show them a character who has life beyond those scenes as well.

CHAPTER 11

THE GUEST STAR AUDITION / THE MULTI SCENE AUDITION

The purpose of the Guest Star is to be the vehicle through which the writer presents that week's challenge to the Series Regulars. Some Guest Star roles are large and appear in many scenes. For roles such as these, the character not only delivers the story challenge, but *grows* along with it, *changing* as the story deepens. These changes will push the Series Regulars into more action as they attempt to resolve the problems of the story. The audition for such roles will almost always have more than one scene so that the Producers can see if the actor understands and has the ability to deliver the "arc" of the character and story. Sometimes these arcs will be extensive, such as a character starting out pleasant and ending up a mean S.O.B. Other times their arc will be much more subtle. But there will always be a growth arc to the multi-scene Guest Star roles and the actor's job is to see and portray it.

WHAT A WORLD

Just as it is imperative to know the world of the show when you read for a Series Regular role, it is the same when reading for a Television Guest Star role or any size role for that matter. The advantage you have when reading for a Guest role is that unless the show is brand new, you're able to view an episode or two of the show before the audition. Do not skip this step.

What is the *world* of the show? Is it primarily a geographically based world such as a deserted island or the beaches of Florida, or is it a smaller location-specific world such as a police precinct or an aircraft carrier in a war zone. How do the Series Regulars act in this world? Do they move through it relatively smoothly or are they in constant conflict with the world?

WHERE DO YOU FIT IN?

Is your Guest Star role part of the show's normal world or are you an outsider? A visiting doctor in a Medical Procedural may be new to the particular hospital of the show but the world of medicine is his normal world so he wouldn't be as much of a fish out of water as a wealthy gentleman brought into a Police Precinct to learn about an embezzlement scheme of one of his employees.

Do you control the world or does it control you? A man robbing a liquor store has a gun therefore has control of his world at that moment, whereas the store clerk being robbed has no control.

How does your being in this world affect the Series Regulars? Do you *bring in* conflict or are you there to *help* resolve a conflict?

WHERE WERE YOU AND WHERE ARE YOU GOING?

As a Guest Star you're only around for one, maybe two episodes. Since the Guest Star is closely connected to the story's conflict, it is imperative that the audience gets a clear picture of who a Guest Star character is as quickly as possible so that they can better understand how the conflict affects the Series Regulars. To do that you need to have a clear picture as to where you were *before* this particular conflict in this particular world happened. Were you even in this world or did this particular conflict thrust you into it? The script will have some exposition to give the audience a little of this information but it isn't enough by itself. It is essential that you bring into the scene a strong sense of Where you were before this conflict occurred so that the audience understands as quickly as possible *your connection* to the story's conflict and how the Writer wants them to *perceive* you at the beginning. Are you friend or foe?

STYLE AND TONE

Every show on Television has its own style and tone and it is important that you be aware of both when going into an audition.

STYLE refers to the *way the stories are told*. Some Police Procedurals are very straight forward, focusing on facts and clues and the puzzle of the crime to be solved each week. Others tell their stories through the personal interactions with the Series Regulars by personalities clashing and/or coming together to result in the eventual solving of the crime. In either case, understanding the style would let you know *how* the Writer is using the Guest Star role in this show. In the straight-forward style you might be there primarily to deliver pieces of the crime puzzle. In the more personality-driven style your demeanor might be more important as it could trigger the intuition of one character and lead him in the right direction to solve the crime.

TONE refers to the *manner and quality* of the show. The straight-forward Police Procedural might be very dry, even lacking in much overt emotion. Another show could have a darker, serious quality. The personality-driven show could be much lighter, almost playful, even when dealing with something as serious as murder.

Whatever the Style and Tone of the show, you have to understand it so that your audition presents them with choices that fit into their show's way of telling its story.

GUEST STAR SIDES
SCENE 1 – STARTS ON PAGE 3 OF SCRIPT

EXT.   SHANTYTOWN STREET – CONTINUOUS

The truck bounces along the dirt road and makes a sharp turn into what would be considered an alley in a city. Here it's little more than a dirt rut.

INT. TRUCK - CONTINUOUS

Lucy grips the wheel, fighting to keep control of the truck as it bounces off rocks and muddy holes. Max is in the back of the truck, desperately trying to keep the stacked boxes from toppling over.

                    MAX
          Take it easy!

                    LUCY
          Are they still behind
          us?

Max peers around the boxes out the back of the truck bed. The jeep is not there.

                    MAX
          No. I think we lost
          them. But I can't tell
          there's so much dust
          in the air!

The truck bounces out of the alley and into a small plaza. A few children scurry away, disappearing into several of the shanties. A cloud of dust off to the left catches Lucy's attention as the front of a vehicle whips into the plaza.

                    LUCY
          Oh no.

The vehicle stops.

EXT. PLAZA - CONTINUOUS

But it's not the jeep. A four door pick
up skids to a stop a few yards from Lucy
and Max. The dust whirls around both
trucks, like a thick fog. Through the
haze the shapes of several men emerge as
they approach the truck.

JAMES, 30s, hair the same color as the
beige dust, steps up to the truck. His
military bearing, and weapons, all scream
out American.

                    JAMES
          You all right?

                    LUCY
          Thank god, you're
          American! A bunch of
          locals tried to cut us
          off and...

                    JAMES
          What the hell are you
          doing out here all by
          yourself?

                    LUCY
          I'm not by myself.

Max pokes his head forward.

                    LUCY (CONT'D)
We're with Doctors
Without Borders. We
were supposed to meet
up with the rest of
our group at the
river. The road was
washed out so we came
around from the other
side.

                    JAMES
You drove through Bu-
huato?

                    LUCY
We skirted around it.

                    JAMES
That whole area is
nothing but armed
gangs. You do know
they kill, kidnap and
confiscate anything or
anyone stupid enough
to go anywhere near
it.

                    LUCY
We had no choice. We
have to get to Lofa.

                    JAMES
What's in the back
there?

                   LUCY
           Medical supplies,
           medicine.

                  JAMES
           You think it's still
           intact after crashing
           along these roads?

                  LUCY
           I hope so. They're
           very well packed. Can
           you help us?

                  JAMES
           Of course. Why do you
           think we're here?

Four men step up behind James. Each carries an AR 15.

              JAMES (CONT'D)
             (to his men)
           Load 'em up.

The men walk to the back of the truck and rip back the canvas top and grab boxes.

                  MAX
           Hey! Leave those
           alone.

Max yanks a box out of one of the men's hands. Suddenly an AR 15 is inches from his face.

                    JAMES
I wouldn't argue if I
were you.

                    LUCY
What are you doing?

                    JAMES
I just told you Bu-
huato is full of
gangs. Not all of them
are locals.

                    LUCY
You can't do this!
People will die with-
out this medicine.

                    JAMES
Open your eyes, doc.
People are dying over
here with or without
your medicine. You
can't save them.

                    LUCY
Oh, so I should become
like you, a mercenary?
A thug with a gun?

JAMES
Funny, cause I see my-
self as just a guy
trying to make a liv-
ing, same as you. We
both came to this pit
of a country because
the taking is easier
here. You save a few
people, you'll be a
big hero get some
fancy position at a
hospital back home. No
one will know how many
you killed.

LUCY
I haven't killed any-
body!

JAMES
No? What do you think
happens five minutes
After you leave a vil-
lage? Guys like me
come in, take all the
stuff you left and
kill anybody who's a
witness. That's a lot
of people dead because
of you. Me? I don't
kill anyone; unless I
have to. Now, both of
you get out of the
truck. Slowly.

Lucy looks at Max. There's nothing they can do but comply.

SCENE 2 – STARTS OF PAGE 42 OF SCRIPT

EXT. – VILLAGE – CONTINUOUS

The five remaining Drassi gang members are firing heavily on the church, empty-ing their guns, chunks of plaster and wood flying off the walls.

INT. – CHURCH – CONTINUOUS

James fires in short spurts, two of which take out fighters. Lucy and Max huddle in the back of the church. Stevens rushes in from the back.

> STEVENS
> Cap'n, they're comin'
> up on the back. We
> keep 'em firing,
> they're gonna run
> outta ammo.

> JAMES
> Keep'em playing.

> James lays down more
> fire. He jerks back as
> a bullet slams into
> his left arm.

> JAMES
> Damn it!

                    LUCY
          James!

Lucy scrambles forward to him.

                    JAMES
          Get back!

                    LUCY
          You've been shot.

                    JAMES
          And so will you if you
          don't get down. It's
          not the first time
          I've been shot.

                    LUCY
          And it's not the first
          time I've been shot
          at. Max, throw me that
          rag and the screw-
          driver!

Max throws Lucy the rag and screwdriver.

                    LUCY (CONT'D)
          I need to get a tour-
          niquet on this now.

Lucy quickly makes a tourniquet.

                    JAMES
          Why doc, I thought
          you'd be celebrating
          me taking a bullet.

>   LUCY
> I came here to help
> people, not watch them
> die. And that even in-
> cludes you.

>   JAMES
> You're something, you
> know that?

>   LUCY
> Yeah, well so are you.

A pick-up truck pulls up, the bed filled
with gas cans and ammo boxes. A militant
riding in the back hops down, hoisting an
RPG rifle. He struggles with it as another militant breaks open an ammo box.

>   JAMES
> I think their ammo
> just got a boost. Ste-
> vens, can you clear
> out the back?

>   STEVENS
> Oh yeah.

Stevens fires nonstop out the back, killing the two Drassi men firing from behind
the truck.

                    JAMES
Doc, get back there.
When I give you the
word, you, your pal
and Stevens are gonna
make a run for the
truck.

                    STEVENS
What are you gonna do?

                    JAMES
Get them to waste
their ammo.

                    STEVENS
Cap'n, there's still
time for you and me to
get outta here. Give
boy wonder here a gun
with a couple of bul-
lets. We can slip into
the jungle and be
gone!

                    JAMES
And give that scum all
those meds? No frig-
gin' way.

                    STEVENS
Cap'n...

                    JAMES
I'm not arguing!

James picks off the militant holding the RPG. Another one rushes up to grab the weapon from the dead man.

> JAMES (CONT'D)
> Doc, what are you waiting for? I told you to get back.

> LUCY
> And you told me you didn't give a shit about me or my mission.

> JAMES
> I don't. But I'd rather you and your dyin' kids have the meds than the animals out there.

> LUCY
> But why don't you and Stevens just take off like he said?

> JAMES
> Can you shoot this gun?

> LUCY
> I can't even lift it.

> JAMES
> Exactly. Go. Now!

Lucy looks at James.

                    LUCY
           My god, there is a hu-
           man being under all
           that crap.

                    JAMES
           Yeah, well you better
           go before the crap
           takes over.

                    STEVENS
           What about you?

                    JAMES
           I'll meet you at the
           bridge. Get outta
           here!

Lucy scrambles to the back. Stevens opens
the door. It's clear. He signals for Max
and Lucy to follow. Lucy pauses at the
door. She looks at James.

                    LUCY
           You take care of your-
           self.

                    JAMES
           Always do. You do the
           same, ok? You can't
           save everybody.

                    LUCY
           No, but I can try.

```
James laughs. He and Lucy hold each
other's eyes for a moment, then Lucy runs
out.

                    JAMES
           How 'bout some fire-
           works for their send
           off.

James aims at the gas cans in the back of
the Drassi truck. He fires and the gas
cans explode.
```

I gave this scene to one of my students, Eric. He read the scene with Dan, who read the other parts as a Casting Director would in an actual audition.

KEVIN: Eric, tell me about your prep.

ERIC: for Scene 1

WHERE - a country in Africa,

WHEN - during a civil war and WHEN my men and I find some easy loot to take.

WHY - I'm here to make money, and these medical supplies will be easy to sell.

WHO - I'm a mercenary, a guy who loves to fight and take what I want.

STORY WHY - from the story point of view, I'm here to interrupt Lucy's plans.

KEVIN: Let's just look at Scene 1 for now and what you've prepped so far. Your reading was good, but a little forced. And I think that's because your prep work was light. Did you do any research on this show?

ERIC: It's a new show, so nothing has aired yet.

KEVIN: That doesn't mean there is nothing out there about it. Did you go online to see what you could learn about it?

ERIC: No.

KEVIN: Well if you had you'd have found out a lot of information like who's in the cast and what the premise for the show is. No Television show exists in a vacuum today. There will always be some information available, even if it is only the sides for the other guest characters in the episode for which you're reading. You'd be surprised how much information you can find in sides for other characters.

You came across really trying to be forceful and intimidating. Now you're fairly well built, not a slight guy. But even if you were smaller, you wouldn't need to play intimidating. Look at what the sides say. First of all, what do the sides tell you about your character by using the all caps punctuation of your name?

ERIC: That it's the first time my character appears?

KEVIN: Exactly. When a name is in all caps, it means the first time we see the character. Even though the subsequent description is brief, it is quite telling, especially compared with the other information the side gives you in the dialogue and in the second scene. You're described as having a *military bearing and weapons.* Not one weapon, but several. So even though you're wearing a t shirt and not packing any weapons right now, at least I hope not, everyone involved in the production of this episode knows how you'll appear onscreen. If you see someone who is extensively armed, do they need to do anything special to appear threatening? Especially if they have a "military bearing?"

ERIC: That's why I wanted to come across as someone you don't mess with. A fighter. You said it was important that the audience knew as much about who I was as quickly as possible, so I wanted to be a guy you don't mess with.

KEVIN: But you came across as someone *trying* to be tough, not someone who *was* tough. To me military bearing says a guy who has extensive training in combat, who knows his weapons, and has the *confidence* to know how to use them in any situation. Someone who is ready to fight when and if needed. All you need to do is be *confident*. And if you take into account what happens in the second side, you'd know you're extremely capable. You can fire a gun with deadly aim, even after getting shot; a gun that Lucy couldn't even lift! Your look is already doing half the work for you. If I look at you and imagine that you're armed to the teeth, I'm already scared. If you put on your "don't mess with me look" it's overkill.

How do you see Lucy?

ERIC: She's an American with an American dude, both harmless. Easy pickins'.

KEVIN: That's it? Do you know who's playing the part of Lucy?

ERIC: No.

KEVIN: That information is available online. A very attractive actress, which is usually the case for Series Regulars. Yet when you read with Dan, you reacted to his Lucy as if the character is merely someone for you to trample on. This guy is in Africa, out in the badlands, chances are he hasn't seen a lot of attractive American women for a while. I'm not saying you need to ogle over her or lick your lips, but she is attractive. The scene isn't about you trying to pick her up, but you can't ignore her either. I guarantee you this scene would play out entirely differently if Max were the only one in the truck. So, not only is she a woman, someone you could easily overpower, but she's an attractive one. That's not going to stop you from taking her supplies in this scene, but we have to see some sort of recognition of who she is in your eyes. You were dead, like a warrior robot.

Whenever you have a scene between two people, especially a man and woman, unless one is a parent or much, much older or younger, a sexual tension of sort has to exist. Sometimes this tension is blatantly obvious, other times not so much. Doesn't mean you don't do what you set out to do, but you do it with your insides acknowledging who Lucy is; especially for a major Guest Star part such as this one. By the end, in the second side when they are looking at each other, saying good-bye, I can just imagine both would be thinking, "Hey, another time, another place, under different circumstances..." That is what makes a full person. No situation is one dimensional.

You're an attractive guy. The actress playing Lucy is going to see that. That's why they brought you in. If they wanted a nerd, they'd bring in a nerd. They very well may. A good Casting Director will bring in all shapes and sizes so the Producers have choices in how they want to cast and tell the story. You have to be confident in who you are and what you are and allow all of that to be part of your audition. That is one of the reasons you were called in.

Another clue that you're not just a hard-assed mercenary is the second side. You do have a conscience, though it may be buried down deep somewhere. Or maybe Lucy is the one who brought it out in you. In any case, though you don't expose it in the first side it is there, behind your eyes. Having that conscience as part of your inner life would have allowed you to be firm in the first scene without being such a robotic hard ass. The way you came across in the first scene, the second scene wasn't believable, especially with no other material given to you as to what has happened in between.

This is an important note here. You were only given two scenes, one at the beginning of the episode and one at the end. The two scenes were opposites in how you treated Lucy. So you can bet that there are a number of scenes in the middle where something happens to you to bring you to the place where you act like a hero in the end and not a sociopath. Most probably Lucy happened to you. She's a doctor who's volunteered to take herself into Hell on Earth so that she can help people. She's also the Series Lead. Chances are she got to you. For that to happen, there has to be something in your character, however small that allows you to be affected by her. If you played the first scene with a little more of this in mind, you still would have been a tough guy and taken Lucy and Max hostage, but you wouldn't have come across as an immovable piece of granite. Just because the second scene hasn't happened yet, you can't ignore any information it gives you about who and what you are before it does happen.

Give me your prep for the second scene.

ERIC: WHERE, a church, pinned down by gunfire.

WHEN, during a gun battle;

WHY, I'm fighting for my life. I don't want to die!

WHY from story perspective, I have a chance to save Lucy and Max, and I do.

KEVIN: I like your Story Why but your Character Why is slight. You're not only fighting for your life, you're fighting for Lucy's and Max's lives as well. By saving Lucy *and* her medicine you get a chance to show her you're not such a bad guy after all. That is an important part of who James is, not just from a story perspective, but from the actor's perspective. Yes he's a mercenary, but he isn't without a conscience. You played it instinctually in this scene, but I think if you had acknowledged it and written it down in your Prep work for this scene, it might have affected your first scene. Even if you didn't go back and add that quality to your first scene's written Prep work, because you identified it in the second scene most likely you would have subconsciously added it to the first scene. If you had done that it wouldn't have seemed so absurdly out of place for you to save Lucy and her meds in the second scene. The way you played it, you were such a robot in the first scene that the guy with feelings and the potential to be "human" in the second scene came out of nowhere.

This whole story, from Lucy's perspective, is to basically let her know that in this world, nothing is necessarily what it seems. This script is from one of the first episodes. You know that because the show hasn't even aired the pilot yet. Lucy is newly arrived in this environment so she's just learning about her world, as is the audience. That is important for the Guest Star actor to know, as it clues you in as to what your job is. In this episode, it is to make sure

Lucy is prepared for anything and that everything in her world is fluid.

WORKSHEET FOR GUEST STAR ROLES

To help you fill in your Story Prep Work, you have to go further than just obvious material in the sides.

1- THE WORLD – Describe the world of the show? Is it a big location, like a city, or is it narrower, such as a high-powered law firm in a major global center?

2 - HOW DOES THIS WORLD NORMALLY PROCEED? Is it a place of constant turmoil, such as a County Emergency Room or is it more evenly paced?

3 - IS THIS A WORLD YOU NORMALLY INHABIT? Are you normally a part of this world, such as a cop from another precinct helping out on a case or are you a visitor to this world? How does being in this world affect you? Do you like it or would you rather be somewhere else?

4 - WHAT IS THE TONE AND STYLE OF THE SHOW? Most of the time a Guest Star character needs to fit in with the tone and style of the show, but there are rare times when he is an obvious counterpoint to it. Know how you fit in to the telling of the story.

5 - WHAT IS THE CONFLICT of the story and HOW ARE YOU RELATED TO IT? Did you *bring* it in or were you brought into this story *because* of it?

6 - WHO ARE THE SERIES REGULARS you interact with? Even if you don't directly interact with them until the end of the

show, or at all, who are the Series Regulars most *affected* by the conflict?

7 - HOW DO THEY NORMALLY HANDLE CONFLICTS? Do they resolve them fairly easily, such as a policeman solving a crime or does each week's conflict bring in major life-threatening obstacles, such as a world of Zombies or Vampires?

8 - HOW DOES THE CONFLICT IN THIS STORY COMPARE WITH OTHER CONFLICTS IN OTHER EPISODES? Even if you've only seen one other episode, how does this conflict compare?

9 - WHAT ABOUT YOUR CHARACTER IS SPECIFICALLY INSTRUMENTAL IN PRESENTING THIS CONFLICT? Is it a physicality, such as hardened soldier coming up against unarmed doctors or is it intellectual like a criminal who is always one step ahead of the detectives?

10 - WHAT ABOUT YOUR CHARACTER IS SPECIFIC TO THE RESOLUTION OF THE CONFLICT? The resolution of the conflict will almost always be brought about by the actions of the Series Regulars, but what about you enables them to do it? Are you active in the resolution or is the conflict resolved despite you? In the Doctors Without Borders scene, based on how Lucy has affected him during the show, James actively saves her and her medical supplies. In another show a criminal's cockiness and mistakes might lead the Series Regular to resolve the conflict by arresting him.

CHAPTER 12

THE TELEVISION CO-STAR AND FEATURED PLAYER AUDITION

Now let's look at this piece as a Co-Star audition side. Take Scene 2, the part of STEVENS.

If the Guest Star's purpose is to either thrust the Series Regulars into a different world or show them a variation of their own world, the Co-Star's purpose is to help *qualify* that world, much like an adjective or adverb in a sentence. Neither an adjective nor adverb is the star of a sentence nor is either one the object. They are descriptors. The *tall* man spoke *loudly* to the gathered audience. *Tall*, the adjective, and *loudly*, the adverb, fill out the picture of a man talking to a group of people. Such is the role of the Co-Star; it is a *Supportive player, a clarifier of the story.*

This doesn't mean Co-Star roles aren't important; merely that they are rarely the central focus of a scene. As such, it is essential that the actor reading for a Co-Star role know exactly how the part for which he is reading supports the main thrust of the scene and/or episode. The Co-Star role often is present to give the Series Regulars more or new information about their world, but rarely does the Co-Star dramatically interrupt their world or send them in a different direction. If this does happen, it is almost always more because of the information they have shared rather than the force of their personality and/or who they are.

But just because a Co-Star role is smaller doesn't mean that you don't have to do any homework. You still need to know as much information as you can about the show. At the very least you need to know the World of the show along with the Style and Tone. After all, if your job is to help *clarify* the story, you need to *fit into* the story.

I gave this scene to several actors to read for the part of Stevens. I am going to take two of these readings and examine them here, because they were both complete opposites and both underlined the two most common mistakes most actors make when reading for a Co-Star role.

The first actor to read for Stevens was Andrew.

KEVIN: Ok Andrew, tell me about your prep work.

ANDREW:

> WHERE: In a shack in the middle of the jungle in Africa.
>
> WHAT: I'm in a gun fight with a bunch of guys.
>
> WHEN: In the middle of a firefight.
>
> WHY: I'm getting shot at, so I'm firing back.
>
> WHO: I'm a hired gun.
>
> STORY WHY: We've got to keep the main characters alive.

KEVIN: Like Eric's prep work in his first scene, it's a little slight, particularly your What and Why. Everything you said is accurate to a point, but it didn't really do much for you because you left out some major elements. You said the lines properly, but I didn't really feel you were in a firefight in a shack in the middle of a jungle, or anywhere for that matter.

ANDREW: Well you pointed out that the Co-Star isn't the focus of the scene, so I didn't want to make it the "Stevens the Mercenary" story.

KEVIN: Exactly, Stevens isn't the focus of the scene but he is an essential part in depicting the desperate and deadly situation. If the audience doesn't feel that every single person in this scene is at risk of imminent death, there is no story. So while you can't steal the spotlight, you have to fully present the reality that while James and Lucy are taking a few moments to reveal more about themselves to each other and the audience, a fight with life and death consequences is taking place. Your entire body was filled with an almost everyday energy, as if this was just another day in your life.

ANDREW: But it is just another day in my life. Stevens is a mercenary, so he does this every day.

KEVIN: He *still* does this everyday precisely because he doesn't *treat it* like it's just another day. Have you ever been in the service?

ANDREW: No.

KEVIN: You play any sports now or in school?

ANDREW: I played a little football in high school.

KEVIN: Your team win or lose?

ANDREW: A little bit of both.

KEVIN: Did you always play at the top of your game, give it 110 per cent every game?

ANDREW: Of course not; especially a game the day after a party.

The class laughs, as do I.

KEVIN: All right. Now think back to one of those games after a party. Can you tell me about it?

ANDREW: Yeah. We went out and played. Everybody's energy was down, but it was no big deal. My school team wasn't that great, not like we were division champions or anything.

KEVIN: Do you think it would have been a big deal if everyone on the winning team was going to be given a new car?

ANDREW: Oh, Hell yeah.

KEVIN: How about if instead of playing against high school kids in shoulder pads and helmets you faced a bunch of hardened criminals with knives and guns whose sole intent was not to win the football game, but to kill you; every one of you, then everybody watching in the stands.

ANDREW: I... I guess I'd be a little more focused.

KEVIN: If you weren't you wouldn't be here to wonder about it! Yes, this man is a mercenary, and yes, he probably gets in firefights most days. But the reason he is alive is that he stays focused and on high alert in *every* fight. And that's just from Stevens' perspective. Take this fight from the Story's perspective and it is even more dramatic. Lucy and Max don't get into firefights every day and probably have never been this close to a violent death before. Therefore Lucy and Max, as well as the audience, are going to look to you and James to gauge just how serious this situation is. Your energy needs be high enough to make us feel the tension of fighting for your lives without stealing the focus. You need to be primed for battle in every second of this scene, much like a cobra striking then rearing back to see when and where it needs to strike again. You don't have much to say, but that's not only because the scene isn't about you, it's because your job is to have James' back. If he wants to talk to Lucy, your job is to make sure no one sneaks up to the house and kills everybody while he and Lucy are having a little tête-à-tête. By looking at this scene as another chance for you to be killed instead of simply as an everyday occurrence, your energy will be amped up enough so that when you speak, it will be efficient and focused, because you can't waste a second of time. It will be just the accent the scene needs to emphasize the real danger everyone is in.

You fell into the trap of *underplaying* in order to guarantee you wouldn't steal the focus of the scene. Just because a Co-star role isn't the focus of a scene doesn't mean that the role isn't important or that the role can be approached with anything less than a full commitment. Your WHEN, WHAT and WHY were so bland that it's no wonder you underplayed the scene. Instead of your WHEN simply being "in the middle of a firefight," how about "trapped in a shack, surrounded by enemies shooting at you with no way out except to clear a path by killing enough men to escape." For your WHAT, if, instead of simply "in a gunfight with a bunch of guys," you had written "fighting for your life against well-armed force who outnumbers you," you would have more fully connected to the severity of the scene. And by changing your WHY from, "I'm getting shot at so I'm firing back," to something like "I will be killed if we don't win this fight," you will even further connect to the commitment necessary for you and everyone else in the scene to survive.

CONNECTION AND FOCUS

There are two elements of any audition that are mandatory and they are *Connection* and *Focus*. CONNECTION means you are *fully connected to this human being in this situation in this time and place*. You may be a mercenary who is fighting yet another battle while your leader, the main Guest Star and a civilian, the Series Regular Lead, play out the scene but you are 100 percent necessary to the success of this scene. By living this scene like it was just another day at work you not only did not *support* the scene, you *detracted* from it; you *disconnected* from the life and death reality instead of *connecting* to it. Your casual prep work led you to a casual connection. You behaved as if you were merely firing on someone because they happened to be firing upon you. Do you see how this connection did *not* support the scene?

ANDREW: Yeah, I do. I guess I was so afraid of doing too much that I didn't do enough.

KEVIN: That's a common mistake many actors make when approaching the Co-star audition. It's a fine line between not doing enough and doing too much but a line that can easily be managed if you read the scene carefully and fully understand *how* the Co-star role supports the scene. Once you understand that you'll know just how far to go to properly connect to the role and focus on the particular circumstances so that you truly support the scene.

The second essential element of any audition but particularly the Co-star audition is Focus. FOCUS is what you *do* with the connection. I'll discuss that more in depth when I address the second reading of this scene.

The second actor reading for Stevens was Frank. Unlike Andrew's rather subdued reading, Frank's was overly supercharged.

KEVIN: Frank, tell me you prep work.

FRANK:

WHERE: I'm in the middle of dense jungle in Africa, in a hut.

WHAT: I'm blasting away at a group of militants bent on killing us.

WHEN: We're surrounded by guys with major artillery, we need to get out now.

WHY: If we don't escape, we're all going to die.

WHO: I'm a soldier, a killer, the last line of defense.

STORY WHY: If James and I don't save them, Lucy and Max will die.

KEVIN: Ok, that's pretty intense stuff. You connected to the severity of the situation very well. I felt as if you believed your life was on the line. The trouble was that your Focus was off. You were so invested in the idea that you had to save everyone from certain death that you became much more than a supportive player.

FRANK: I don't understand. I only had a little bit of dialogue compared with James and Lucy. But we're being shot at, I've got to know that what James wants me to do is the right thing or we're going to die and the few lines I have is the only time I can get that out.

KEVIN: Yes but you were *so* intense, so *insistent* that James completely explain himself and almost *force* you to follow his orders that you created a whole different scene than the one written. Suddenly it became a scene about a possible mutiny. Yes, you're in a fight for your lives and the ability to figure out the best course of action is paramount if you're to survive, but that decision rests with your leader, James, not with you.

Most of your prep work was good, but you see the difference between your Story Why and your personal Why? Do you see that this scene is about so much more than just your ability to fight and save your life? It's about James coming to the decision to risk his own life to save not only yours but two relative strangers' lives as well. It's about Lucy seeing that James is not as two dimensional as she thought and realizing that her world is not so easily definable as she believed it to be. In order for the Story Why to be served, James has to be allowed to make his self-sacrificing decision without distraction. He is your leader, he has probably made decisions you didn't agree with in the past but the fact that you're alive and kicking means those decisions worked.

The Writer created your dialogue with James not because he wanted to showcase you standing up for yourself and questioning your orders, but to show the audience that James is making a decision that is contrary to what everyone expected him to make. Your questioning him underlines the possibility that this decision may bring about his own demise. This is necessary to create the sacrifice that produces the moment of revelation by Lucy; that this man is more than just a robot soldier. By you being so focused on forcing James to defend his decisions to you, you re-directed the focus of the scene; you put it on you combating your leader and not on the clarification of his decision.

This is why it is essential that when reading for a Co-star role you understand how that role fits into the *whole puzzle*, not just from your perspective. By being so intent on demanding that James explain his orders you added a whole other element to the scene, a whole other set of circumstances. Suddenly the audience has to worry not only about the militants, but now they have to worry about you.

Connection and *Focus* are the two most important aspects of the Co-star audition. You have to be *connected* to the material fully and have the correct *focus* so that you don't upstage the story, but instead contribute to and support it. Correct Focus can only be achieved if you understand how you *fit into* the story and know what is *necessary from you* to tell the story as written.

THE FEATURED PLAYER/ONE-TWO LINE AUDITION

The Television Featured Player is most often a one or two line role. Sometimes it has a few more lines, but the job of this role is simple; populate and represent the world of the story at that moment. Look at Chapter 8, The One or Two Line Film Audition as the information regarding the One or Two Line Television audition is the same as it is for a film audition. This role is there to fill out the world of the story.

CHAPTER 13

THE TELEVISION COMEDY

The Television Comedy Audition is similar to the Episodic Television Audition, but also different and unique unto itself in many ways.

The breakdown of the Roles, their importance and part they play in telling the story is pretty much the same as in the Episodic Television Audition. The Guest Star is still the one who brings in or represents the main conflict or conflicts each week, the Co-Star is still a modifier, and the Series Regulars are the ones who solve or try to solve the problems. The fundamental difference is in the TONE of the show, TYPE of problems, and HOW the Series Regulars go about dealing with the problems.

STYLE AND TONE

Though every Television show has its own Style and Tone, they are most evident in Television Comedies. This includes everything from how a show is lit, to what colors are used primarily in the sets and costumes, to what kind of stories are told and how those stories are told. Though it is advisable for actors auditioning for *any* Television show to be aware of as many of these tonal elements of the particular show as possible, it is *critical* when auditioning for a Comedy. They may be similar but every comedic show has its own feel and its own way of being funny. Some are very broad while others are extremely subtle. In some comedies the characters behave like clowns while in others they are like anybody you'd meet on the street. In order to successfully audition for a comedy, you *must* know the Style and Tone of the show. To reiterate what I said in Chapter 11, STYLE refers to the *way the stories are told* and TONE refers to the *manner and quality* of the show.

SERIOUS STUFF

There is an old saying, "Comedy is Serious Business." I'm not sure who first said it, but it is true. What that expression means is that though what is happening in the story is funny to the audience, *to the characters involved* it is serious business. Whatever problems arise in a Comedy are generally of a fairly light nature. No one is seriously ill, nothing has truly life or death consequences. Someone late to the office sales meeting because he can't find his pants, or everyone bringing a turkey to the family potluck Thanksgiving are typical Television comedy storylines. Neither one is a truly a life or death situation, but they might be to the characters in the story. Not all characters in all comedies view the possible outcomes of any problem with such dire possibilities, but they all take them as serious obstacles to the life they wish to lead.

LIGHTEN UP!

In comedy negative emotions are softened somewhat. A character may not be *angry* as much as he is *frustrated*. Someone won't truly *hate* another character as much as want to *win* something while that other character *loses* it. In Single Camera Comedies the emotions involved are closer to real life than broader forms of comedy, but they are rarely, if ever, purely negative.

Here is where the Tone of a comedy show comes into play. The severity of the reactions and the way the characters try to solve the problems are unique to each show. In one show it just might seem like the end of the world if little Sally doesn't make it in the school play and everybody's life is thrown into chaos in order to make it happen. In another it might be more of a challenge and the other characters don't throw their lives into chaos as much as they adjust them in order to surmount this challenge. If you've never seen an episode of a Comedy you're auditioning, do so. No matter how faithfully your best friend can recount every episode to you, it won't be the same as actually seeing show.

PACING

Any discussion of comedy would not be complete without mentioning pacing. In general comedies are paced faster than dramas. Slow isn't funny. That doesn't mean you race through comedy, just that you don't dwell on anything too long. People speak, there is a reaction and a response, almost always without too much time in between. Pausing is rare in comedy, and if it is present, it has to brief and full of unspoken words. Knowing the pacing of a particular show is important to successfully auditioning for that show. Usually pacing is pretty apparent in the writing, but nothing beats watching an episode or two.

COMEDY ARCHETYPES

Archetype is a word that is thrown around quite a lot, especially in writing courses all over the world. "In order to tell a story successfully you must have the archetypes!" is a chant heard over and over from one writing course after another. Sometimes they are referred to in terms of mythology or from examples of classic Greek and Roman drama, other times they are names from medieval literature and other times they are characters right off a classic television show. This may seem completely ridiculous when discussing Television comedy. After all we're not talking about epic tales of vanquishing legions of foes or battling the enemies of the gods, we're talking about someone burning the holiday dinner or forgetting to buy milk at the store. But story archetypes, especially comedy archetypes, have survived the millennia for a reason: they not only help make a story funny, the audience loves them and continuously *seeks* them in any show they watch.

Archetypes are characters that traditionally have specific attributes and play particular roles in a story. Their use in story telling comes from the audiences' universal, perhaps even unconscious, knowledge and acceptance of who these characters are and how they navigate through the world. For example the *Hero* is an archetype who appears in every story. He is exactly who the label implies, someone whose goal is to "save the day" and make the world a better place for everyone. Heroes come in all shapes and sizes, some are likeable, some are not, some are young, some are old. The Hero of a show or an episode may be any character. It may be the same character week after week, or it may be a role the characters of a show all share, depending of the storyline of any given week. But it is a role that is always taken on by one or more characters. Without any of the characters assuming the role of the Hero, there would be no resolution to any story because no one would take the necessary actions to resolving it.

Every one of us recognizes a Hero, whether we consciously know it or not, and this recognition makes it much easier for us to become involved in a story. It is easier because every time we encounter a show or story we are encountering a new world. In order for us to fully enter that world and allow ourselves to become engaged in the story we seek familiar structures, like reaching out for a stairway banister; something to grab onto to give us an instant recognition of where we are and what is going on. An archetype is a familiar face in a new crowd.

Whether you realize it or not archetypes are present in every story, dramatic and comedic, from ancient Greece to last night's Sit-Com. But in comedy they are much more evident for a simple reason: they save time. The faster an audience recognizes who the players are and what the dynamics of their relationships are, the faster the audience gets the jokes. In today's world where a Television Comedy is usually 30 minutes, you need to hook the audience into the world of the show as fast as you can.

This doesn't mean that every comedy will have the same characters played the same way all the time. Some stories will have just a few simple archetypes, others will have many variations. And though each story will hopefully have characters that are fully unique to its particular show, the roles the characters play in delivering the comedy will be inevitably linked to one or more traditional archetypes. Your job is to identify which ones.

There are many books discussing and defining long lists of comedic archetypes, but there are about five basic types that appear in all comedies. Not every comedy or every episode will necessarily have all five present at any given time, but when reading for any comedy you need to identify which archetypes *are* present. Doing so will help you find the humor of the story and how it plays specifically in the show.

1- THE PLAIN JANE or JOHN - This character is not necessarily plain looking. What I mean by Plain is they are fairly neutral. Most likely the conservative of the bunch, they are not going to go too far in any direction. Their physicality will be pretty straight forward, as will their verbal interaction with the other characters. They are the anchor, the post that remains fairly constant while the other characters swim around them. In traditional comedy this part is called the Straight Man. Much of the humor might be at their expense but they are still the glue that holds everyone together. This character is usually the Lead, frequently the title character of the show. This character is also most often the Hero.

2- THE COMMENTER – This character is the dry, sarcastic voice. He or she makes jokes about any and everyone else in the show. Not mean necessarily or combative, more like someone who stands on the sidelines shaking their head and making cracks about all the insanity going on around them. They are usually above getting their hands dirty in any situation but they are all too eager to tell everyone else how wrong they are in these situations. They can be cutting in their observations or simply offer a wry social comment. Their physicality is generally the lowest of any of the characters because their humor stems from their observations more than their participation. Occasionally the Commenter will take on the role of the Hero, but not often. They are more observers than doers.

3- THE MEANY – This is the one who is constantly confronting one or more characters. Whereas the Commenter will offer an aside as to what someone is doing wrong, the Meany will come right out and tell them to their face. The role of the Meany is to provoke and bully the other characters. The Meany does this successfully with everyone except the Commenter, who is usually above being easily provoked. This clash of personalities can be the source of much humor as the other characters scurry around reacting to the Meany's pokes while the Commenter simply stares at the Meany and doesn't budge. A word of caution regarding The Meany. This character has to be mean, *to a degree*, but cannot be without some humanity and love, however deeply these attributes might be buried. Many comedic characters, even entire shows have failed because the Meany was without mercy or redemption, simply downright evil. Their job is to *provoke*, not annihilate. A too heavy-handed Meany isn't funny and will destroy the audience's desire to tune in. The Meany might be the Hero of a story, but very rarely. It is their job to stir up trouble, not fix it.

4- THE DINGBAT – The Dingbat is always in his or her own world. Many times this character is physically quite different from the other characters, geeky, nerdy, out of shape, or the exact opposite, a bombshell; at least in comparison to the rest of the cast. They may actually be dim-witted or just someone who sees things around them in a manner no one else does. Often the butt of the joke, the Dingbat never really gets the joke, even though he is the star of it. The Dingbat is a constant source of amusement for the audience because the Dingbat is a constant source of irritation for the other characters. Every now and then the Dingbat is the Hero of a story, which comes as a nice surprise because it gives the Dingbat a depth that is not usually seen week to week.

5- THE BUFFOON – The bumbling one not afraid to do or say anything, no matter how dumb it makes them look. Frequently physically larger-than-life than the other characters, but not always. It's more the Buffoon's personality and penchant for saying anything at any time that gets him into trouble and gets the laugh. The Buffoon is constantly upsetting everyone's world, though not maliciously. He just can't sit back and watch, no matter what is going. If there is a catastrophe in the story, usually the Buffoon is at the center of it. No matter what their intention, if something can go wrong, it will go wrong for the Buffoon. Every so often the Buffoon is the Hero, despite most likely being an integral part of any week's particular dilemma.

These are just five Archetypes, but they are the most common personalities in comedy. Some shows may have characters than combine two or more of these personalities. When you read a comedy script, look to see how any of the characters fit into this list. In some shows it will be very obvious; in others it will be much more subtle. But every comedy will have some combination of two or more of these Comedic Archetypes.

CHAPTER 14

THE SINGLE CAMERA COMEDY AUDITION

As I mentioned in Chapter 8, the Single Camera Comedy is not filmed in front of a live audience. It is much closer in tone and style to the Episodic Television Drama than a multi-camera comedy show. The main differences are the Tone of the show and the Style of the writing.

THE SINGLE COMEDY SERIES REGULAR AUDITION

If you're reading for a pilot you won't have the opportunity to view any episodes to see the style and tone of the show, so you have to find them in the script. This is one of a number of situations where the Casting Director can be your very best friend. If you're not sure of the tone, if it isn't clear to you from the script just how the Writers and Producers intend the comedy to play, *ask*. Most Single Camera Comedies are not too over-the-top in terms of the performances but they will differ from show to show in how the characters *focus* in terms of solving the problems. Are the characters intent on fixing whatever is wrong with single-minded purpose and tunnel-vision, or are they more laid back in their approach? Is the comedy coming from opposites, does one character view the situation as total bedlam while another sees it as a small bump in the road? Whatever the case, the comedy will stem from the need to get the problem solved and ways the characters go about solving it. In Single Camera Comedies, more often than in Episodic Dramas, one or more of the Series Regulars will introduce the problem instead of a Guest Star, with the Guest Star, if there is one, being part of the problem.

The Comedic Archetypes I listed in the Chapter 14 are present in Single Camera Comedies but they are often not clearly evident as being one archetype over another. Quite frequently the Series Regulars of a Single Camera Comedy possess the elements of more than one Archetype, and depending on the story of a particular episode, one Archetype is more dominant than another for that episode.

In the Single Camera Comedy Series Regular audition, *Identify* the problem, who brings it and make specific choices as to *How* you are going to deal with the problem based on the script and your own uniqueness. What Archetype is closest to your character? If it is more than one, which one is more prevalent in this particular instance? Are you the Buffoon who is taking on the role of the Commenter in this case? Are you the Plain Jane or John who makes a Buffoonish mistake? Make the character your own by understanding the Archetype the character plays in the series, the role he plays in delivering the comedy of this script, and infusing the character with your own personality traits that fit this Archetype as well as the Tone and Style of the comedy.

Series Regulars return each week, so if a character seems to be much larger-than-life, look for a place where he or she isn't; look for the *balance*. It may come in the form of character combinations. One character may over react to everything while the partnering character may under react, giving the situation balance. You must understand how your character contributes to the overall comedy and you must play your part.

An important difference between the Single Camera Comedy and other broader comedies is how they are filmed. Unlike Dramatic Episodic Television, rarely will Close-Ups be used in Single Camera Comedies. But Single shots are used a lot and the focus is closer than in broader comedies. That means the audience is closer to you. Because of that, the humor is more subtle than in a broad comedy. Single Camera comedies are often an hour, twice the time of the broader Sit-Com. In an hour long show a Series Regular is given more time to struggle with *how to respond* to a dilemma, rather than having to just jump to an immediate response. In fact the struggle with how to respond may hold more humor than the eventual response. But like any comedy, by the end of the show there will be some sort of resolution.

Single Camera Comedies generally have softer resolutions, more "feel good" moments for everyone involved rather than splashy endings. But in order to "feel good," the character or characters must have "felt bad." In Single Camera Comedies the humor comes from watching the characters struggle to "right" the thing or things that made them feel bad in the first place.

TWO ESSENTIAL ELEMENTS OF THE COMEDY AUDITION

In any show all characters combine as parts to make a whole. But in comedy the specifics of *who* the characters are and how their *personalities* combine to make a whole need to be clearly defined. Understanding precisely *how your character fits into the combination* is one of two essential elements for a successful comedy audition.

The second essential element is *Chemistry*. Chemistry comes from the way you interact with other characters and manifests itself in the tension or ease your combined personalities produce. Chemistry is not something you can really prepare or work on; it will naturally occur when you're paired with another actor. But by understanding how your character plays into the creation of the comedy you'll put yourself in a place where meaningful and productive Chemistry with another like-minded actor is more likely to happen. By knowing which Archetype(s) your character embodies and which one(s) the other character(s) in the scene embody, you will have a good clue as to the kind of chemistry needed between the characters in the scene for the comedy to work.

THE SINGLE CAMERA GUEST STAR AUDITION

As with the Episodic story, the role of the Guest Star in a Comedy is the same; he most often brings in or represents the problem of the week. With *most* Single Camera Comedies, the Guest Star roles will be fairly straight forward as they are bringing in an everyday life situation which the Series Regulars will see as a serious impediment to life as they know it. But once again, Chemistry is an important part. If the Guest Star role interacts with a character who is generally larger-than-life, most often the Guest Star role will be the opposite, very low-key and matter-of-fact. If the Guest Star brings the problem to a more laid back character, the Guest Star role may have a larger personality and/or that larger personality might be the problem.

This is not a hard and fast rule so read the sides carefully to see just where the comedy lays. There are times when an over-the-top character is confronted with a Guest Star role who is just as over-the-top and when a laid back character is coupled with a Guest Star role that is also laid back. In such situations the comedy will often lie in the clash of personalities as much as whatever problem has arisen. Whatever the case, the Guest Star actor has to know the tone and style of the show along with specific nature of the comedy of the episode for which he is reading.

There might also be times when the problem of the story is created by the Series Regular and the Guest Star is merely a part of the problem or the person representing it. It is imperative in such scripts to identify what the specific problem is for the Series Regular character and how this Guest Star role represents it or makes it worse. In scripts such as these the Guest Star isn't necessarily the problem, just proof that it exists.

An example of this might be a story where one of the Series Regulars complains that no one listens to him. Enter the Guest Star in a scene where he doesn't listen to the Series Regular. The job of the Guest Star here is to simply present evidence that the problem exists. The problem isn't the Guest Star, Mrs. Jones, it's that the Series Regular character feels *no one* listens to him; the *Series Regular has created* this problem by making it universal. Mrs. Jones is merely an example of how he feels the whole world reacts to him.

This is quite different from a story where the Series Regular declares, "Mrs. Jones never listens to me." Now, *Mrs. Jones* is the problem, whether real or perceived; the Series Regular is simply announcing it. In this case the character of Mrs. Jones would have a reason not to listen to the Series Regular and thus would be a stronger personality than a guest character in the first scenario who is but one among many who don't listen to this character. In this scenario, Mrs. Jones is the problem, not merely a representation of it.

Once you understand whether your Guest Star Role is the problem or simply a representation of a larger problem, examine the script to see where the comedy or jokes are and how they play. In Single Comedies, the jokes are usually presented in two parts.

Part One: a character says or does something.

Part Two: another character reacts by saying or doing something in response.

Though both have comedy in them, generally the Part Two is the bigger laugh. This back and forth can go on for an entire scene or just a few lines, depending on the show. It can include many characters or only one if the character is reacting to discovering a letter or some other such solitary thing.

The Series Regular will almost always have the biggest laugh in any comedy exchange. Again, this is not a hard and fast rule so you have to read the script carefully. But most of the time, the Guest Star is the catalyst for a comedic reaction from the Series Regulars. The Guest Star is a set-up so the audience will laugh at the Series Regulars' antics to deal with whatever problem is thrown at them. But occasionally the Guest Star or even a Co-Star is part of the pay-off of a joke. Take the Mrs. Jones example.

SERIES REGULAR A: I'm telling you that woman never listens to me.

SERIES REGULAR B: Oh, you're just being paranoid.

SERIES REGULAR A: Really? Mrs. Jones the building is on fire!

MRS. JONES: That's nice.

The final part of the pay-off is the Series Regular A's *reaction* to the proof of his problem, but Mrs. Jones is the first part of that pay-off.

If you're reading for a show that is on the air, do your research. Which Series Regulars are in the scene and which one are you setting up? How have they dealt with problems in previous shows? Most of the times in comedies, the Series Regulars deal with very similar problems show after show. Therein lays much of the comedy; as the audience gets to know the Regulars, they can anticipate how they will react to many problems and will start to laugh at the set-up, since they have an idea what reaction is most likely to follow. Most of the time the set-ups in comedies are already established and consistent. By knowing as much as you can about the Series Regulars in your audition scene, you will know how they typically react to similar situations and set-ups. This is a big clue as to how Guest Star Role fits into the story. Knowing the set-up and comedy delivery style of the show and the Series Regulars is imperative.

THE SINGLE CAMERA COMEDY CO-STAR AUDITION

The Co-Star's purpose in a Single Camera Comedy is the same as the Episodic Story, a modifier or mild accent to the scene. Most of the time the Co-Star roles in a Single Camera comedy will be straight-forward, but occasionally they will be more *charactery*. It will all depend on the particular show and the particular story that week. By understanding the Tone, Style and Pace of the show, along with identifying where and how the comedy in the scene lays, the Co-Star actor will see how he fits into the story.

Look for the comedy. Though the Co-Star Role is generally a smaller part of a bigger problem, it is frequently part of a comedic set-up. You should do as much research as you would if you were reading for a Guest Star Role as the requirements for a successful set-up of the comedy are the same. You have to know what the joke is and who is delivering it in order to set it up properly. The Co-Star role can be as large as a whole scene or as small as one word. But it is there for a reason, *to participate in a joke*. It might be a small, very subtle joke, but by identifying what the joke is you will understand how your role contributes to it. Are you a brief interruption or a major support? What do you need to do for them to get the laugh the way they routinely get it?

WORKSHEET FOR SINGLE CAMERA COMEDY AUDITION

1 - WHAT IS THE WORLD OF THE SHOW?

2 – WHAT CHARACTERS ARE THE SERIES REGULARS?

3 – WHAT ARE THEIR ARCHETYPES?

4 – WHAT IS THE STYLE OF THE SHOW? IS THE COMEDY BROAD OR SUBTLE? IS THE COMEDY PRIMARY PHYSICAL OR VERBAL?

5 – WHAT IS THE TONE OF THE SHOW? IS IT LAID BACK OR EDGY?

6 – WHERE IS THE CONFLICT AND COMEDY IN THE SCENE?

7 - WHAT IS YOUR ROLE IN THIS CONFLICT? DID YOU CAUSE IT OR DO YOU ONLY REPRESENT IT?

8 – WHERE ARE THE JOKES IN THE SCENE AND WHAT IS YOUR PART IN THEM? ARE YOU PART OF THE SET-UP (MOST OFTEN) OR ARE YOU PART OF THE PAY-OFF?

CHAPTER 15

THE SIT-COM AUDITION

THE SIT-COM AUDITION

The Situation Comedy, or Sit-Com, is written and filmed like a short play. It is filmed in front of a live audience, or made to look like it is with a laugh track added to make it seem like there is an audience. In Sit-Coms the characters are generally much broader than in the Single Camera Comedy. They pause for laughs and the characters mostly face forward, towards the audience, as actors on stage do. The set is also much like a stage set, with a definite front, sides and a back.

THE SIT-COM SERIES REGULAR AUDITION

In reading for the Sit-Com Series Regular, do your homework. Who is involved with the writing and producing? Has the Writer created or written for other Sit-Coms before? If so, what was the style of those shows? How was the comedy presented? Was it very broad humor or was it a little more subdued? Was the comedy primarily physical or verbal? What got the laughs? Who is the Producer? What has he or she done before? Same questions as with the Writer, what kinds of shows has this Producer done and how did the comedy play in those shows?

188 Kevin Scott Allen

Once you've done your homework, what is going on with the specific show you are reading for? What kind of world is it? The same Prep work you would do for the Episodic, with an added layer being that of the show's comedic style. An example of this might be found in your *Where*. A scene's *Where* might be: "your apartment." A *Series Where* coupled with a *Style Where* might be: "your apartment where your neighbors enter through the front and back doors any time of day or night without knocking and without seeing it as wrong it no matter what you're doing at the time." That suggests a pretty fairly broad style with an old fashioned *schtick*, or recurring gag, of people entering a scene at any time without warning. The persona of someone living in such a place would be different from someone who lived in a more traditional household where non-residents knocked, or at least called hello from an open window before entering.

Once you've identified the Style of the show, look at the specific comedy in the script. How does your character fit into the comedy? What is the Archetype of your character? Are you the straight man, the more subdued of the piece or are you broader and more flamboyant, the one with bigger reactions?

Archetypes in Sit-Com are much more evident and pronounced than in the Single Camera Comedy. Part of the reason is that the humor in Sit-Coms is broader than in the Single Camera show. Another reason is time. Sit-Coms are generally a half an hour, which means if you allow time for commercials, only 22 minutes of actual show; not long. Therefore the easier it is for the audience to identify any character's role in the comedy, the quicker the jokes will fly.

A Sit-Com episode is written as a series of small jokes all leading up to a final pay-off at the end. Typically there are three jokes per page. These jokes may be stand-alones, in that though they contribute to the comedic flavor of the overall show, they are not necessarily part of the main problem that week, or they may be part of the main problem. But whatever their purpose in that week's story, they all serve to *amplify the personalities* of every character in the scene and, through the humor, re-enforce those personalities.

Almost all Series Regular characters in Sit-Com's are extremely self-centered. Not in a negative malevolent way; they mean well their needs are just more important than anyone else's. The world revolves around them and their problems. Therein in lies most of the comedy, with all of the Series Regulars competing with each other and their world to be the most important being around.

YOU AND YOUR OWN FUNNY BONE

This is where you and all your uniqueness come in. Comedy is about tension. Nothing is funny if everything is all wonderful, if everybody gets along and nobody has a problem with anybody else. The humor in Sit-Coms particularly comes from how a group of people with usually opposite personalities, *who can't leave*, get along. When I say can't leave, I don't mean physically unable, though that might be true in an episode from time to time. I really mean don't really *want* to leave for some reason; they're all family, or friends who feel and/or act like family, co-workers, all *co-dependents* of some sort. And there is a reason they don't want to leave, no matter how apparent or strong the animosity between any of them appears to be: *deep down, they need to be together.* Like any true co-dependent, life without the other or others is worse than life with them. As I said earlier in this chapter, negative emotions in comedy are softened. In the case of antagonist characters, it's more that they love making fun of each rather than they honestly dislike each other. To leave would deprive them of a sparring partner. And most probably, deep down, there is love for each other, no matter how buried beneath verbal jabs. I say verbal jabs because in comedy rarely does anyone get seriously physically hurt. Again, true pain isn't funny.

As you read the Sit-Com script, what characters are your sparring partners? What is the reason you spar with them and what is the reason you stay around? Do you need to be here because of a job, or because of a sense of family obligation? Do you have no other place to go, at least no other place that would be better than here? Find your own character's reason for being in a place where week after week it will be a battle of the personalities. How are these other characters written and what about who you innately are is the opposite of that, either physically or personality-wise? It doesn't have to be whom or how you are most of the time in your daily life. You may normally be a delightful, upbeat person but from time to time a caustic, sarcastic side blurts out which might be the perfect foil for another character in a Sit-Com script. Bring that part of you to the audition. You can be all nicey-nice when the audition is over, but if the bitchy part of you brings out the humor in the scene and produces a comedic tension between the characters, let it out. How the characters react to and off each other can and will be fine-tuned when it comes to Chemistry reads, but long before then you have to bring some sort of chemistry to the initial auditions when it's just you and the Casting Director or a reader. By understanding where the comedy lays in terms of characters' interactions, you will be one step closer to a Series Regular role on a Sit-Com.

SIZE DOES MATTER

The size of a performance is extremely important when reading for a Series Regular Role in a Sit-Com. Though Sit-Coms vary in performance size, with some delivering characters whose performances are much larger than others, in pretty much all Sitcoms, *all* characters are larger in life in one way or another. Their world is usually such that any normal person would run from it. The fact that they not only stay in but seem to thrive in it takes a person who is larger than life in some way. But that doesn't mean all characters in Sit-Coms give *over-sized performances*. If the style of the show is more realistic, the performances in general will be more realistic. But the performance styles could very drastically, even within in one show. Depending on the Archetype and how the comedy is written some characters may be over-sized while others are extremely subdued. By finding the jokes and discovering what makes them funny, you'll find the key to the size of the performances.

RHYTHM AND TEMPO

With any comedy, but particularly Sit-Coms, the writing of any show has its own, unique Rhythm and Tempo. This is something you can identify if you do your research. Along with the type of comedy the production team has produced in the past, what have the Rhythms been in those shows, and do they appear to be the same in the script you have now? Comedy writing is like music; rhythm and tempo are integral parts. Often times more than the actual words, the rhythm and tempo are what make a scene funny. Are the jokes all one-liners, one after another, or are they longer sentences?

LOOK FOR THE THREES

Sit-Com comedy jokes are typically written as sets of threes.
Part One: Set-up for the joke
Part Two: Reaction to the set-up joke.
Part Three: Pay-off joke.

Or

Part One: Set-up for the joke.
Part Two: Second set-up for the joke.
Part Three: Pay-off joke.

Look for this format in your script; it will be there. By identifying these three parts of the jokes, you will find the rhythm of the comedy. A common comedic rhythm is:

1- a sentence or two of set-up

2- followed by a *briefer* sentence of a reaction to the set-up, or further defining the set-up

3- followed by an *even briefer* sentence, or even just a word, of a pay-off, or final reaction to the set-up and first reaction.

By identifying *how* the joke works, you'll find the tempo. Does the joke rely on anything physical, such as a look or gesture to work? If so, where does this physicality occur; in the set-up, the reaction or the payoff? What kind of physicality is it? Is it broad or subtle? This is an important part. A physicality that is too big or too subtle will ruin the joke. Larger-than-life characters tend to have larger-than-life physicality's, but be very careful that any physicality you choose enhances a joke and doesn't overshadow it. The writing, the style, the rhythm, tempo and pace, along with the character's persona, will all give you clues to the perfect size physicality. Physicality in comedy is simply a pay-off or punch line that is a physical reaction to the set-up instead of a verbal one. For a punch line or pay-off to work, it needs to be sized appropriately to the set-up and situation.

If there is no obvious physicality in the joke, is there room for one? Is there any kind of physical movement that might either cap the joke or give it an extra punch and dimension? It can be something as small as a raised eyebrow or as big as spinning around and making a grand exit. It must fit in with the style and tone of the show as well as the style and tone of the character. But look for places where some sort of physicality will support and enhance the joke. But be careful not to put in a physical gesture just to do it. It has to support what is written. If a gesture appears to take away from the written joke or make the joke about something else, don't do it.

FILMING STYLE

Just as with the Single Camera Comedy, the way a Sit-Com is filmed indicates a style and manner of performance. Because it is presented in a format similar to a play, the shots on a Sit-Com are mostly very wide including several, if not all, the characters in the scene. This is especially true in the Set-up, with the shots becoming narrower with each part of the joke. The pay-off is very often a single shot of the character delivering the pay-off. But the single shots are not quite as close as with the Single Camera Comedy, allowing for a broader performance than the Single Camera Comedy.

Because the Sit-Com is much shorter than the Single Camera Comedy, the characters don't spend much time mulling over a problem. They form a game plan to fix it and act on the game plan as quickly as possible. It may take a couple of plan changes to get to a resolution, but a Sit-Com is about what the characters do to fix a problem and not as much about how they feel about the problem. Sure they have feelings about what's going on, they just don't dwell on them very long without doing something about it.

MIND YOUR P'S AND CUES

Sit-Coms are filmed using multiple cameras all filming at the same time. Because of that, when you're in a scene in a Sit-Com a camera is on you, whether you're speaking or not. Therefore your Performance has to be there one hundred percent, all the time. You never know when the Director might want to switch to you for a quick, two second reaction shot, even in a conversation in which you say nothing. If you're there, unless you're obviously not part of a conversation and not supposed to even be hearing it, you're on camera.

That is also why it's essential you pick up your cues. Pausing is DEATH to comedy. That doesn't mean you have to speak the second another character stops. The *occasional* Pause can be quite effective in comedy, if it is full with intent. A comedic Pause is merely a brief moment when you're speaking very loudly with your mind and not your words. But your mind must be speaking.

In a Sit-Com the Director is not on the floor with the actors during the filming of the show. He or she sits in a booth, watching what every camera is getting and switching to whatever camera is giving him the coverage he wants for any particular moment in the show. Because the show is being edited as it is being performed, the pace has to be *efficient*. Lag too long in responding, and there will be a big hole of dead air. Sure this can be fixed in a pick-up shot later, but the performance will never be quite the same as the one you gave with the audience present or during the run of the entire scene. So Pick Up Your Cues.

But beware of picking up your cues *too* quickly. If you come in right on top of a cue or, worse, overlap and speak over another actor, there is no way the director can cut from a camera covering the group to one covering only the actor speaking. Comedy works because there are exactly enough words in the set-ups and pay-offs of the jokes. If you overlap another actor, some of those words won't be clearly heard and the joke won't work.

YOU'RE THE ACTOR, NOT THE WRITER

The same is true if you add words of your own. You'll not only throw off the rhythm of the joke, you could make it completely un-funny. Sit-Coms are timed down to the second. A writer has about twenty-two minutes in a half-hour Sit-Com to deliver as many jokes as he can fit in. The writers have watched the actors rehearse the show to see which jokes work and which ones don't. They have modified the script accordingly, adding here and taking away there. If you start adding your own words or bits to the show, no matter how great you may think they are, they will alter the timing. The jokes won't work the way they were planned and if you add too much the show will be too long. In a world where advertisers pay a lot of money for a thirty second commercial, if each scene runs over by a couple of seconds, by the end of the show you've lost one or more commercial time spots. So if you want to add words get a job as a writer. Otherwise make the words you've been given work.

CHAPTER 16

THE SIT-COM GUEST STAR AND CO-STAR AUDITION

THE SIT-COM GUEST STAR AUDITION

In auditioning for a Guest Star Role in a Sit-Com, as with the Single Camera Comedy, you must know the world of the show and the Series Regulars in it. Though Sit-Coms are closer to each other in Tone and Style than Single Camera Comedies, they are still unique unto themselves. The world of one may be zanier than the world of another. In one Sit-Com the Guest Stars may appear each week to bring in "the problem," whereas in another Sit-Com the very natures of the Series Regulars and their relationships to each other produce enough problems of their own so that the Guest Stars are there to reinforce one side's view of the problems against another's.

Watch several episodes of a show for which you're auditioning. Watching one episode will give you a sense of the Tone and Style and an idea of the Archetypes, but if you watch more than one episode you'll be able to see patterns. Is the problem in the show you're reading for a typical one or is it new? Is it a problem for the same character or characters as it has been in the past? Are they reacting to this problem the same as they have in shows past or are they trying a new tact to solve it? By learning as much as you can about the show and its comedic patterns, you'll better understand how the writers intend for your Guest Star Role to fit in to the comedy.

Know the Archetypes of the Series Regulars in your scene or scenes. Are you there to support their activity or to counter it? Did the Meany bring you in to knowingly create havoc while he sits back and watches delightfully, or are you an innocent bystander caught up in the game?

THE GUEST STAR AS ARCHETYPE

Are you taking on the role of one or more of the Archetypes? If you remember my example about Mrs. Jones from Chapter 12, I listed one scenario where a Series Regular makes the observation that "Mrs. Jones never listens to me." If this is the case in your audition is Mrs. Jones The Meany in this episode? Or is she The Dingbat and just doesn't understand what the Series Regular is saying to her? Or are she merely part of a problem set up by another Series Regular?

As with the Single Camera Comedy, the Sit-Com Guest Star is almost always part of the set-ups for the Series Regulars to get the pay-off laugh. This is not to say the Guest Star Roles aren't supposed to get laughs. They are often given pay-offs of their own. But in a Sit-Com the final laugh is pretty much always given to the Series Regular, especially if the Guest Star Role is not a recurring one. Even if the Guest Star has the last line in a scene, the pay-off will undoubtedly be the Series Regular's reaction to that line. If the Guest Star role does turn into a Recurring Role, the last laughs may switch back and forth. But a typical Sit-Com Guest Star Role will bring in a problem to force the Series Regulars to act to fix it and through their actions, the Series Regulars will get the biggest laughs.

FITTING IN

The *size of a performance* is extremely important when reading for a Guest Star Role in a Sit-Com. What are the sizes of the performances in general on the show? Is it made up of Series Regular characters that are *significantly* larger than life? Is only one of them larger than life? As I noted in the previous chapter, all characters in a Sit-Com are larger than life in one way or another. But not all Series Regulars demonstrate that in every episode. What is the normal size of the performance for any Series Regular who is in your scene? Does the comedy come from you matching their performance size or from being quite different from it? Do you sit passively while a Series Regular rants and raves about something or do you give it right back to them? If you do give it right back make sure what you do doesn't completely eclipse them unless that is expressly written.

BE STRONG BUT NOT OVERPOWERING

The Guest Star Role in a Sit-Com is generally an antagonist to one or more characters, though they may be right in sync with the other characters. The comedy will come from those antics the antagonized characters do in order to react to and overcome that antagonism. Therefore you have to be strong enough to present a challenge but not so strong as to be completely insurmountable. If you are an immovable wall, not only will your being overcome be unbelievable, nothing about the situation will be funny. Remember, emotions and attitudes in comedy, especially Sit-Coms, are softer than in Drama. A Sit-Com Guest Star Role whose character presents a major obstacle should possess an attitude that will be more *smug* with the power they *think* they hold rather than being dangerous and oppressive.

A good way to determine the attitude of a Guest Star Role in a Sit-Com is to compare the role and the scene to a Drama. If it were a Drama, what would be the serious consequences if the Series

Regular did not respond correctly to whatever problem the Guest Star brings in?

Let me give you an example from my own experiences. Some years back I was rehearsing an episode for a Sit-Com where I was one of the Guest Stars. In a particular scene, one of the Series Regulars was arrested for something and was thrown in jail. I was also in jail and this scene was about me terrorizing the Series Regular, amplifying his need to get out of jail fast. I approached him slowly and with a cold menace, and at the end of the scene he was visibly shaking. After running the scene, one of the Producers came up to me and the Series Regular. He complimented us both on our acting but said it was too real. He told us that watching the scene, he actually became afraid that the Series Regular's character's life was in jeopardy. He wanted us to lighten it up a bit. I looked back on what I had been doing and realized that I had been playing the scene as genuinely threatening to the Series Regular and he had been reacting accordingly, as genuinely frightened. So I took my threatening "I'm gonna kill you if you don't do as I say" attitude and made it more of a pompous strut, an "I'm king of this cell and you're my play thing" attitude. The scene went from frightening to funny, and the Series Regular was able to get a big laugh at the end of scene from a look of comic desperation instead of real desperation.

By finding the Dramatic attitude of the scene first, I was then able to lighten it up.

THE SIT-COM CO-STAR AUDITION

The Sit-Com Co-Star Audition requires the same prep work and research as the Guest Star. Though your part is smaller, you still have to fit into the specific world of the show. As we discussed in Chapter 9, in the Dramatic Episodic show the Co-Star role is most always there to reinforce what is happening in the world around the Series Regulars and Guest Stars. Rarely does the Sit-Com Co-

Star bring in something new to that world and if he does it is most often just information and not the force of his character.

But in Sit-Coms it is quite common for the Co-Star Role's personality to be part of a joke and not merely an information presenter. Like the Sit-Com *Guest Star*, the Sit-Com *Co-Star* can be a set-up to a joke by presenting the Series Regular with a problem. The difference is that if the Sit-Com Co-Star Role does have this job, the problem is brief and usually does not produce more than one or two jokes.

If your scene involves your role setting up the Series Regular for a joke, look at the scene carefully. What is the set-up? Is it information only or is it also a specific personality trait as well? If the scene takes place in a library and the Series Regular tends to be loud, is it merely the words "Be Quiet!" from the Co-Star Role of a Librarian that provide a set-up or is it also a stern, no-nonsense demeanor that chastises the Series Regular with a look and enables them to get a laugh by their reaction to this small Meany character?

By knowing the Archetype or Archetypes of all the characters in the scene, including the possible Archetype of your Co-star Role, you will be better able to identify all the elements of the humor and see what is needed for the set-up. A Co-star Role is not there to steal the laugh, but to support it. So if a large personality is part of the set-up, make sure this personality is large enough to deliver the set-up but not so large as to hijack the joke.

CHAPTER 17

TELEVISION REENACTMENT AUDITIONS

THE REENACTMENT SHOW

The Television Reenactment Show is a very popular genre and uses a large number of actors each season for the simple fact that every story is a portrayal of a real and specific event that involved real people. If the audience is to believe the actors in any segment of a show are representing real people, these actors can't be in more than one episode. If they are the audience might not buy into the illusion that the characters on the screen are real people. Therefore the Producers are looking for a full cast of new actors each episode.

Nearly all Television Reenactment shows are improvised during filming as well as during the auditions. The actors will be given information regarding a particular scene. Sometimes the information given is very specific, such as a scene between a victim being held up at gunpoint inside a store. Other times the information will be general, such as two people meeting at a new hire orientation. But whatever you are given, your job during the Reenactment audition will be to *create a scene that comes to life*. Let's discuss how to do that.

CRIME IS THE NATURE OF THE BEAST

The Crime Reenactment Drama involves a crime or crimes. For these shows, the roles cast usually fall into four categories:

1 – Victim
2 – Perpetrator
3 – Witness and/or Friend of the victim
4 – Law enforcement personnel

IN YOUR OWN WORDS

There is generally never a traditional script for Crime Reenactment Dramas. The information you receive will vary from show to show. Some will give you an elaborate Story Board where each shot of a scene is written out like a cartoon with text describing what happens in each shot while others will only give you a paragraph or two of information. The information will be about the crime, who your character is and how you are connected to the crime, whether you're the Victim, the Witness, the Perp or Law Enforcement. You will be expected to improvise a scene from the story, most often with other actors auditioning for the other roles.

For Reenactment Dramas, as with everything else, doing your Prep Work is ESSENTIAL. There is generally no scripted dialogue to help you, so you must use every tool at your disposal to help you pinpoint the specifics of the WHERE, WHAT, WHEN, WHO and WHY.

When casting a Crime Reenactment Drama the Producers usually look for actors who resemble the real people involved. If you are called in for such a character, you have to do more than just look like the character you're reading for. You need to DO YOUR RESEARCH. What, if any, information is available on the internet about the real event? Does this information mention your character? What does it say about them? Does it reveal any personality traits, such as a combative lover or a flustered witness?

If it doesn't reveal any personality traits, what information *does* it give you about your character? If there is no information about your character, what does it say about the crime, the people involved and environment in which it took place? Is it the back woods of Tennessee or downtown Manhattan? Learn as much as you can about the crime and the *world* of the crime. What types of people live in that world? Is it a world where crime happens all the time or one where it rarely happens? If you were to take a trip to that place, what would you do, how would you dress, what would you say to fit in?

Let's take an example of a Crime Reenactment Scenario.

SUMMER, 1991, SANTA MONICA, CALIFORNIA
STACY CARTWRIGHT, 23, had recently broken up with her longtime boyfriend, CARL ANDERSON, 24, and moved from Columbus, Ohio, to Santa Monica. Three months later, Stacy is found shot to death in her apartment.

PAULA, her best friend from Ohio, told police that Stacy broke up with Carl because he was abusive and she moved to Santa Monica to get away from him. Paula said Stacy told her Carl had gotten into drugs and that when he was high he would hit her. He refused to go into rehab and would become violent whenever Stacy brought it up. When Carl was arrested for possession, Stacy moved out while he was in jail. She told no one but Paula where she was going, but Paula is convinced Carl found out where Stacy moved and followed her to Santa Monica when he got out of jail two months later. Stacy told Paula her mother didn't believe that Carl was abusing her, and in fact Stacy suspected her mother of trying to seduce Carl when they were living together.

DETECTIVE NORMAN EVANS was the homicide investigator assigned to Stacy's murder. At the time, he interviewed everyone involved, flying to Ohio to talk to both Paula and Carl. Though he suspected Carl, he could never prove that Carl was in Santa Monica.

CARL ANDERSON swore to Detective Evans that he never hit Stacy and that she moved to California because she wanted to be an actress. He says he tried to talk her out of it, but that she wouldn't listen. He admitted that he had a problem with drugs. At the time of Stacy's murder, Carl had just gotten out of jail and was living on the streets hanging out with a bunch of addicts. He denies ever seeing Stacy again after she left Ohio, but says he still loved her. He asked Stacy's mother, Mary, if she knew where Stacy had gone, but Mary told him she didn't know and that Carl was better off without Stacy. Mary offered to let Carl move in with her, and he did.

Stacy's neighbor, ALAN, 28, told police that Stacy was quiet and kept to herself. He was in her apartment only one time when she asked him to help her hang a picture in her kitchen. Other than that, he rarely saw her.

CONNIE, 47, worked with Stacy at a coffee shop in Santa Monica. She told police that Stacy was going out with a guy she met playing volley ball at the beach. Stacy never told her his name, but she heard Stacy talking on the phone to some guy she called MARK.

MARY CARTWRIGHT, 53, Stacy's mother. She and Stacy never got along. Stacy's father died when Stacy was five and Mary remarried. When Stacy was 16 Mary accused her of trying to seduce Mary's new husband. DAVID. Stacy denied it, but Mary kicked her out of the house. Soon after, Mary's husband left also. Mary told the police she was sure Stacy and David had an affair, but she could never prove it. David died in a car accident when Stacy was 18. Mary never believed that Carl abused Stacy, and told detectives that Stacy was a constant liar. Mary told detectives she never knew where Stacy moved to.

After months of investigations, the case went cold. But Detective Evans never forgot the case. Twenty years later, at the request of Stacy's sister, the Santa Monica police revisited the case and asked for Detective Evans' help. A letter from Carl was found buried in Stacy's things. He had convinced Paula to tell him where Stacy was and he wrote to her, telling her he loved her and would find some way to prove to her that he was clean from drugs at last. Items from Stacy's apartment were checked for DNA. A sample of blood found in Stacy's bedroom was analyzed and found to match DNA taken from Stacy's neighbor, Alan. No DNA was found in Stacy's apartment matching anyone else. When Alan was confronted with the evidence, he broke down and confessed that he murdered Stacy when she refused to go out with him.

I gave this Reenactment Scenario to one of my classes. But before we discuss how and what they did, let's discuss how to do your Prep Work for a Reenactment show.

You approach your Prep Work the same as you do for a scripted Film or Television side. You need to find out as much information as you can and the WHERE, WHEN, WHAT WHO and WHY formula will give you all the information available. But *what you do* with that information will be a bit different. Let's look at the Prep Work as it covers the story generally.

1st DISSECTION:

WHERE – The story takes place in two *geographical* locations, Columbus, Ohio and Santa Monica, California. Within these *geographical* locations will be several specific locations depending on what character's story is being told at the time. Though no specific scenes have been listed in the information given, you can imagine what most of them would be based on whatever character or characters you look at. We will discuss this in more detail when we focus on the specific characters.

WHEN – Generally, 1991 and the present. More specifically, before Stacy moves to California and after she moves to California. A little more specifically, ***pre-death of Stacy and post death of Stacy.***

WHAT – Just the general story for starters. In many Reenactment Dramas the events are told from many different characters' points of view, so the WHAT will change depending on whose viewpoint is being told. But the general actions of the story remain the same no matter whose viewpoint is being highlighted.

Stacy moves from Ohio to California. Three months later she is found murdered in her apartment.

It is essential that when you begin your Prep Work you narrow the WHAT down to the most basic. Throughout the course of the audition you may be asked to approach the WHAT from any number of different points of view. If you become attached to any particular point of view early on it will hinder your ability to be flexible. For example if you decide from the beginning that Stacy *definitely* left Ohio to get away from an abusive boyfriend, it might affect your ability to convincingly improvise a scenario about her leaving Ohio to pursue her dream to become an actress. Narrowing down the WHAT to its most basic gives you a neutral jumping off point which can then be colored by any point of view you're asked to present.

WHO – Who are the specific people in the story? As we discussed above every Crime Reenactment Drama will involve four essential characters. Identify all characters and the categories they fit into. Some may fit into more than one category. A character can be a witness and also the Perpetrator.

1 - the Victim - Stacy

2 - the Perpetrator or Perpetrators – unknown, but Carl is the most obvious suspect

3 - the Witness and/or Friend of the victim – Paula friend and witness to Stacy's Ohio life, Mary mother and witness to Stacy's Ohio life, Connie, co-worker and witness to some of Stacy's California life, Alan – Stacy's neighbor in California, possible witness.

4 - Law enforcement personnel – Detective Evans.

WHY – The WHY at this point is fairly broad. TO DISCOVER WHAT ACTUALLY HAPPENED. To do this the story will be explored from a number of different angles and viewpoints.

2nd DISSECTION:

This time you will do your Prep Work from the viewpoint of your particular character. The point of the 2nd DISSECTION is to uncover as much information as possible as it relates specifically to your character. Let's take the character of Paula.

WHERE – Read the material carefully. What locations would Paula be in, both geographically and specifically? Paula is a friend of Stacy's from Ohio. Nothing says Paula ever left Ohio, so most likely all of Paula's WHERES will take place in Ohio. More specifically, since she and Stacy were good friends, probably one of their homes.

WHEN – Depending on how the story is told, either 1991, the present, or both. You may be asked to improvise the time Stacy told Paula she was leaving for California and/or asked to improvise a scene twenty years later when the case has been reopened and Paula is relating the last conversation she had with Stacy to either Detective Evans or a new detective working the case. More specifically scenes with Stacy could run a range from two best friends hanging out to when Stacy is afraid for her life and she confides in Paula. All scenes with any law enforcement personnel will occur *after* Stacy has been murdered.

WHAT – So far, all you know is that Stacy confided in you that her boyfriend, Carl was abusive and that she was moving to California to escape him. Stacy also told you that she suspected her mother of trying to seduce her Carl. Any improvs you will be asked to do in the audition and/or filming will be for the purpose of presenting this information to the audience. To prepare for this ask yourself questions to fill out the scant information given. To know what questions you should ask, TAKE THE INFORMATION THAT IS GIVEN AND EXPAND ON IT FROM THE CHARACTER'S PERSONAL POINT OF VIEW.

1-Did you know or at least suspect Carl was abusive to Stacy before she confided in you?

2- Did you know about Carl's drug use?

3- Did you know about Stacy's tumultuous relationship with her mother?

4- How do you feel about Stacy moving to California? Was it a good idea to go live among strangers, or do you think she would have been safer if she had stayed close to people who knew her?

Remember any scene you improvise will not only be based on what you bring to it but also on whatever the other actor brings. You must be flexible enough to explore an improvised scene from a number of angles, not just the one you like the best.

WHO – WITNESS/FRIEND OF THE VICTIM. Best friend of Stacy. Someone in whom Stacy confided when she was in trouble and someone who cared about Stacy.

WHY – Stacy told Paula she was leaving Ohio because she was afraid of her boyfriend, Carl. Paula is convinced that Carl somehow found out where Stacy was and killed her.

Paula is an essential element in depicting the possibility that this is actually what happened to Stacy. Stacy also told Paula that she suspected her mother of trying to seduce Carl. So Paula's viewpoint not only points to Carl as the killer, but could portray Stacy's mother as an unreliable witness when it comes to Carl.

THE REENACTMENT IMPROV AUDITION

When you go into an audition, you will generally be paired with another actor. Some actors like to get together before they go into the audition room to try out some improvisations. This is fine as long as you don't lock anything in. You have no idea what you'll be asked to do once in the room and you may be given adjustments that ask you to do exactly the opposite of what you planned. Better to make sure you familiarize yourself with the information about the characters and the particular scene you will be asked to improvise.

Know the relationships.

If you're the Victim, in addition to knowing the relationship between you and the other actors, you need to know *WHEN in the relationship* the scene you're being asked to improvise occurs. Is it when everything is fine or a scene when there is trouble between you and the other characters?

The same applies if you're the Witness. Know the relationships and WHEN they are. Is this when you thought everything was great between the Victim and the Perp or after you suspected trouble?

If you're the Perp, know the relationships, WHEN the scene you'll be asked to improvise takes place, and *especially be sure to know the WHY*, or at least have a definite opinion about it. *WHY* are you forced to commit the crime you commit? Is there anything anyone could do or say to stop you?

If you are Law Enforcement, know who the other characters are and know precisely *how much* you know about them at the specific time of the scene. Is it when you're just trying to figure out who everybody is or is it when you have a pretty good idea who committed the crime? Is it the first time you've questioned them or is a second or third time? Are they a willing or reluctant witness?

DON'T WRITE THE SCRIPT

Many actors, when faced with the improvisation audition, decide they're safe as long as they keep talking. RESIST THIS URGE. You are being hired to create a scene with other characters. *A scene can't happen if you're the only one talking*. A good rule of thumb with an Improv audition is the *STATE/ASK* formula. Make a statement about yourself and then ask another character a specific question. If you're not the first one who speaks and another character has asked you a question, make that *ANSWER/ASK*.

Example:

Character 1: "I'm starving, I'm glad we stopped for something to eat. Have you been in this restaurant before?"

Character 2: "No, just thought it looked like a good place. You know this area?"

It's not a hard and fast rule that each part of this design be only one sentence. The idea is to *create a dialogue* between the characters, not a narrative of one character telling the other what is going on. If you ask questions of the other character, questions that have to do with the story, you'll create not only a dialogue between you and the other character, but you'll get information when they answer the questions. After you answer the question asked of you, if their *reaction to your question* doesn't suggest another question, the *information* in their answer and *their question* to you should. By doing this, as the actors build a dialogue, they build a relationship; and if you know the factual information you've been given about the story, it will be easy to seamlessly slip that information into this dialogue and your relationship will be specific to the story.

EXPOSE YOURSELF AND THE OTHER CHARACTERS

Use your questions and answers wisely. The point of asking a question is two-fold. One, it forces the other character to respond to you, and two, when they answer your question it is an opportunity for them to give you information. If you're aware of the relationship between the characters, these questions and answers should *expose* that relationship. If everything is going on smoothly then the dialogue should reflect that. If you're at a point in the relationship when one of you is questioning the sincerity of the other, let the questions and answers reflect that.

If you use the Improv audition to *expose* the feelings in the relationship rather than to simply tell the story or merely repeat factual information you've been given, you're showing the Casting Director and Producers that you understand the dynamic between the characters. And that dynamic is what they are looking for. If they wanted a definite and specific script, they would have hired a writer. What they want is to see what personality and life you bring to the relationships. You're simply using your own words to show it.

Two of my students got up to improvise an audition for the roles of PAULA and STACY. The scene they were to improvise was the scene where Stacy tells Paula she's leaving to get away from Carl. Rebecca played the part of Stacy and Lisa played the part of Paula.

During the improv both students struggled. They repeated themselves quite a bit and traded paragraphs of dialogue that did little to define or enhance their relationship or the story.

KEVIN: Ok, how did that feel?

LISA (PAULA): Like we were just talking but not saying anything.

KEVIN: Exactly, because that's what you both were doing. Talking without saying anything. I'm going to address you both by your character names to make it clearer what went wrong. Stacy, you began the improv by telling Paula that Carl was abusing you. Paula you launched into a tirade against Carl and also against Stacy, telling her you couldn't believe she had been putting up with Carl's abuse. Paula you completely ignored the fact that Stacy told you she was going to tell you something she had never confided in anyone before.

PAULA: Well I thought it was obvious that she was being abused and that she was hurting herself more by allowing it to continue. I mean I'd seen her with black eyes, how could she think I didn't know?

KEVIN: Where in the material you were given does it say that Stacy had frequent or even infrequent black eyes?

PAULA: Well it doesn't but you said to fill out the scant information so I did.

KEVIN: But you filled it out in such a way that it locked you and your partner into a single viewpoint. In Stacy's opening line she said she had wanted to tell you something, that Carl had *begun* to be abusive. Paula, you ignored the information that Stacy introduced, the information that the abuse by Carl was **fairly recent**. You barged ahead with your own story, the story that you had seen Stacy with countless black eyes. So right from the start, Paula didn't respond to Stacy's information but instead put out conflicting information. The goals in any scene in any story are to reveal information and define relationships. In an improvisation you have to be aware of that even more than in a scripted scene because you don't have written dialogue to help you accomplish those goals.

PAULA: I know, but I've known some abused women and for all of them the abuse had been going on for some time and all of their friends knew long before the women told anybody about the abuse.

KEVIN: That may be, but you are not charged with creating this story alone. You job is to work *with* Stacy to create the story. If she begins with something that is contrary to what you decided, then you have to go with it, or at the very least acknowledge it. You could have said something like, "I was always afraid something like this would happen. I've known about Carl's drug use for a while and felt it was only a matter of time before he hit you. What can I do?" Instead you refused to accept her side of the story and laid down your own. This caused both you and Stacy to pause and stammer a bit, because instead of listening and responding to one another you were trying to figure out what to do with conflicting information.

STACY: That did throw me. Suddenly she was telling me I had been abused for months and I didn't know what to do.

KEVIN: The best thing to do when someone throws a specific, strong and unexpected story "fact" your way is to remember the STATE/ASK formula. Reply with some kind of acknowledgement of the information then ask a question that will help clarify this information for you and give you some idea of how to respond. For example you could have said, "I didn't think anyone knew. How long have you known?" Depending on her answer you can elaborate on the story. Whenever you are in doubt in an improv, or when another actor throws something at you that you didn't expect, ask a question. Most of the time the other actor will respond with an answer that will give you an idea of where to go with the relationship. If Paula responds to your confession with "I've known he's been abusing you for a while," then you can explore reasons why you never mentioned it before, or why Paula didn't say anything about it. By asking questions that spring from what the other actor said you create a dialogue that is based upon two people working together. When you ask a question or make a statement based on a story you created by yourself you run the risk of "story writing." What that means is that you're not working *together* in the improv, but alone.

Another thing you both did is that you both got stuck on only one element of this story, Carl's abuse of Stacy. There is so much more information you could have explored. Paula you just kept repeating your bewilderment that Stacy had endured Carl's abuse, and Stacy you kept wallowing in embarrassment and hurt that you had been abused. Neither of you took the story elsewhere, such as what to do about it. Stacy you ignored the information provided that made moving to California your best option. Your mother kicked you out of the house when you were 16, so going "home" wasn't an option. The fact that Stacy moved across country alone suggests that she did more than just cry about being abused. She did something about it, something that took inner strength. That information suggests that Stacy is fairly strong, but all you did was cry and suffer. Paula, if crying and suffering is the route Stacy took, you also know the information, you could have suggested she move, get out of town and far away from Carl. But you just kept harping on Carl's abuse and so the improv never got off of one note.

An improv audition is much more than thinking of clever lines to say. It is about developing a relationship that moves the story along. To do that you simply have to accept the factual information you've been given and explore it together. But in order to explore you have to listen to each other and allow what the other character says and does to affect what you do and say next.

LETS PLAY COPS AND CRIMINALS

Now we'll look at a couple of the other roles, Law Enforcement and Suspect.

The next two actors to get up were Jason playing the part of DETECTIVE EVANS and Bill playing the part of CARL. Each one spent time doing Prep work, going over the information given.

They were to improv the first time Detective Evans called in Carl for questioning after Stacy's murder. As above, I'll refer to the actors by their character names.

Det. Evans began immediately, asking Carl where he was the night before. Carl stumbled a bit, not sure how to answer. He became uncooperative and a bit defiant. Det. Evans in turn tried to trip him up by jumping all over the place following each answer by Carl with a question that had nothing to do with the previous one or with Carl's answer. The result was two strong personalities who were trying to one-up each other.

KEVIN: Ok, how'd that feel?
DET. EVANS: I feel like I want to slam him in cuffs and throw him in jail.
KEVIN: Why?
DET. EVANS: Because he's a slimy little prick.
The class laughs, even Carl.
CARL: And I want a lawyer right now. This guy's got nothing on me; he's just trying to pick a fight.
KEVIN: And that's about all either one of you did, fight with each other. Det. Evans, you were all over the map with your questions. It didn't seem like you had a plan, or even a clue as to what you wanted from Carl except to get him mad.
DET. EVANS: That was my plan. Get him mad so he'd slip up.
KEVIN: It might be a legitimate police procedure in questioning a suspect to try to throw him off by zipping from a question about one subject to a question about a completely different subject. But doing that in an Improv audition will only show everybody how clever you are trying to be and will not be successful in building a usable relationship between you and the character you're questioning. And usable relationships are essential in any Reenactment show. Your job as the Law Enforcement component is to *guide* the audience through the investigation aspect of the story. In order to

do that you have to find out information so the audience can find it out at the same time. You started out with "Where were you last night?" but before Carl had even finished answering you attacked him, accusing him of beating his girlfriend. Instead of allowing him to answer your question then using his answer to lead you to other questions that *expose* what Carl knows or is willing to reveal, you just jumped on him and tried to get him off balance. By doing that you didn't help expose the story, you got in the way of the story. You made yourself and the combative personality of the detective more important than the actual story. You didn't allow Carl's answers to lead you anywhere. You just decided you would verbally force Carl to admit to *your version* of what happened. That put Carl in a box where the only thing he could think of to do was to yell at you.

CARL: Well he came at me and my natural reaction was to fight back.

KEVIN: That may be, but in fighting back you still could have found a way of doing your job. Your job is to provide information. You just became antagonistic and refused to answer his questions, so you also got in the way of the story.

CARL: What, so I should have just been a wimp who told him what he wanted to hear?

KEVIN: Not at all, but you can't let your characterization take over and eclipse the scene. In a scripted episodic or film story the audience is like a peeping Tom. They spy on the characters' lives as they go on their journey. You still can't produce an overblown character, but you have more leeway to bring a strong character into play because the scripted words will help guide you and the audience through the story. In most Reenactment shows, the audience is almost like a character in a briefing. They are being presented with information in order to explain how a crime was solved or theories of how it went down. Getting them the information is of paramount importance. You don't have a script to rely on, so as actors you have to understand what specific information each scene is supposed to provide. You can bring strong, opinionated characters but you can't block the information unless you've been specifically asked to do so. In this scene both of you just fought with Det. Evans lashing out with accusations and Carl feeling backed into a corner and denying everything.

Remember, the information you were given as to what this scene was to be about was that it was the *first* time Detective Evans questioned Carl. That tells us there will be at least one more round of questioning. So both of you have to create some sort of relationship that will work together to make a second time not only believable but necessary. Detective Evans, if this were such an open and shut case with Carl obviously guilty it wouldn't have been chosen as one of the episodes. These shows are about figuring out "whodunit" when several scenarios are possible. And Carl, you have to at least give the illusion of participating and not just refuse to answer any questions. Defiantly refusing to cooperate makes everyone believe you're obviously guilty and they have no need to watch the rest of the show. You both created strong characters with immovable opinions, but by doing so neither one of you showed that you *understood the story and could improvise in such a way that the story advanced.* These shows don't have much time. You're only one piece of an elaborate puzzle. Each scene has to provide enough information that the show can proceed. So creating a strong character is fine as long as you still provide information. That doesn't mean Carl had to admit to everything the Detective accused him of doing. When someone refuses to believe you're innocent, as Detective Evans did, spend less time challenging him to prove you're guilty and more time explaining why you're innocent.

The LAW ENFORCEMENT ROLE will most obviously be about asking questions.

But you cannot forget the most important job of any actor in any scene, especially an improvised one: LISTEN. It is especially imperative that any law enforcement actor *listens* to the answers to his questions and forms the next question based on what he *hears*. It is vital not to get locked into certain questions or certain opinions of what actually happened. In a true Improv audition, as in real life, you don't know what the other characters are going to say. If the case was solved by the Detective asking only two questions and the Perp confessing immediately, they wouldn't have made a show about it, unless there is a lot more going on in the story than just that. So, as Law Enforcement, your job is to ask questions to find out information you don't know. The best way to do that is to listen and allow every answer you're given to lead you to another, logical question.

As a SUSPECT/WITNESS being asked questions by Law Enforcement, answer according to the information you've been given. Either you're a willing witness or a reluctant one and that information has most probably been given to you. If you're not sure, *ask*. Don't just decide you're innocent or guilty because you think one or the other would be fun and make you more interesting. Your reason for answering the questions and the *way* you answer them should be purposeful in creating a relationship with the Law Enforcement character. Do you want them to believe you? Most likely you do, even if you did the crime or know who did. So, if you're lying, lie well. You can be defiant, if that is what the relationship is, but don't play this attitude so strongly that it gets in the way of the story.

YOUR RELATIONSHIP TO THE STORY

Crime Reenactment Dramas follow one or more characters as the story is revealed, looking at the story from different angles. When Characters form a relationship to the story, the audience knows what angle they're seeing. If you are a Law Enforcement Office who doesn't believe a witness, we know when we see the story from your angle that you're looking for holes in a story. If you're the ex of the Victim, we know we're seeing the story from someone who might be the Perp, no matter what their alibi or claims of innocence are. If you use your Improv audition to stake out a position in the story, you can always be adjusted if it's the wrong position. By staking out a definite position, you bring something specific into the audition room and they get to see who you are and how you could fit into their story. Just don't let your position be so inflexible that you don't allow any other options or refuse to listen and respond to anything anyone else says in the improv that is contrary to the position you took. Maybe you'll hear something that might make you doubt your original position. Maybe what you hear will reinforce it. Either way, start out with a definite position but remain open to change depending on how the improv proceeds.

THE MEDICAL REENACTMENT SHOW

The Medical Reenactment Show is very similar to the Crime Re-enactment Show in that everyone is involved in trying to solve a problem. In the Crime Reenactment Show, it was a crime. In the Medical Reenactment Show the "crime" is the illness or injury.

The usual Character breakdown for the Medical Reenactment Show is as follows:

The VICTIM – the one who is sick or hurt.

The DOCTOR – or other Medical Professional. The job of this role is to treat the Victim.

The WITNESS or LOVED ONE – The husband, wife, significant other, friend or neighbor who is present for all or part of the ordeal.

There is normally no human Perp in the Medical Reenactment Show because the Perp is the illness or injury. If the injury was caused by someone else and that character is part of the show it was most probably an accident and the character who caused it is part of the Victim support team. If they were not supportive and caused the injury intentionally or with malice, then the story would be part of a Crime Reenactment Drama and not a Medical one.

The story in a Medical Reenactment Drama is one where the audience is taken through the steps of curing the Victim. Obviously no story is going to be a simple cure or there would be no point in reenacting it. The drama in the story surrounds the difficulties encountered in making the Victim better.

THE MEDICAL REENACTMENT AUDITION
THE VICTIM

For the VICTIM, know all the information presented to you. Is it an illness or an accident? If it is an illness, how did you contract it? Did it come on you suddenly or over time? What are the symptoms? What happens to you in the course of treatment? Do you survive unscathed or are there long lasting side effects? Who are the other people in the story and what is their relationship to you and to the illness or accident?

In the Improv scenes you have with the Doctor, you'll be asked about symptoms and their severity. Knowing how the illness progresses or how the injury affects you will enable you to use the *STATE/ASK* formula effectively. See the example below under the Doctor's audition information.

MEDICAL PERSONNEL

For the DOCTOR or any MEDICAL PERSONNEL, know all the information presented to you regarding the illness or accident. Is it something you've dealt with before or is this the first time you've treated a patient with this particular malady or injury? KNOW THE MEANING AND PRONUNCIATION OF ANY MEDICAL TERMS PRESENTED IN THE INFORMATION GIVEN TO YOU. I capitalize that sentence because there is nothing more destructive in an audition for the role of a professional than to have an actor mispronounce terms that are fundamental parts of the role's profession. If you're a Doctor you deal in medical terms all day, every day. If you don't *understand* a term in the information given to you, ask or go online to find out what it means. If you don't know how to *pronounce* a word, ask or go online to find a web site that will have an audio presentation of the word. Doctors frequently have to contend with foreign language terms. It is an elementary part of your research to know how to pronounce these terms.

Another element in the Doctor's audition is to know the progression of the illness or injury as presented in the story. Your character's involvement in the story is directly linked to this progression. In any scene you're given to Improv, you have to know where you stand in terms of your Victim's condition and what you're doing about it.

The Doctor's role is much like the Law Enforcement role in a Crime Reenactment Drama. You are trying to solve a problem. You'll be asking questions, examining evidence (medical charts), and reaching conclusions. Like the Crime Reenactment Story, there will be set-backs and steps forward. If you know where you are in the stage of the illness or injury in any scene you're asked to Improv, you'll be able to form your game plan for the Improv. If you're in a scene where the Victim is not responding to treatment, use the *STATE/ASK* formula accordingly.

Example:

DOCTOR: "I've given you a medication (name it if it is listed in the story information) to treat (name the condition or symptoms). Do you have any pain anywhere else?"

VICTIM: "Yes, I have a headache. Does mean the medicine's not working?"

THE WITNESS

For The WITNESS, know the series of events leading up to the medical treatment of the illness or injury and know what your part in it is. Were you there when the symptoms first surfaced or the accident happened? If so, what did you do? If not, how did you come upon the scene? Did you rush to the hospital when you heard your friend/loved one was brought in? The participation of The WITNESS in the Medical Reenactment Improv varies, depending on the story. There are times when the Witness is quite active in the search for the cure, especially if the Victim is unconscious for most or part of the story. It will be the Witness who converses with the Doctor as the Victim can't.

Other times the Victim is able to speak for himself and the Witness is there to add supplemental information. If this is the case, be aware that your role is there to support the dialogue and interaction between the Doctor and the Victim. In such cases you need to follow their Improv, chiming in occasionally when you need to add something someone either forgot or was not aware of.

Example:

DOCTOR: "I've given you a medication (name it if it is listed in the story information) to treat (name the condition or symptoms). Do you have any pain anywhere else?"

VICTIM: "Yes, I have a headache. Does mean the medicine's not working?"

DOCTOR: "Not necessarily, though a headache is not a normal part of this condition. Do you get headaches frequently?"

VICTIM: "Not really."

WITNESS: "About two months ago you had a headache that lasted for a couple of days. Remember?"

VICTIM: "Oh, yeah."

WITNESS: "It was pretty bad, even Advil didn't work very well."

At that point the Doctor would probably ask pointed questions of the Victim but the Witness would have to be on alert to jump in if/when needed.

In the Medical Reenactment Drama everybody is almost always on the same team wanting to solve the problem by curing the illness or healing the injury. Your Improv audition needs to reflect this by working together as a team, all with the same goal of getting the Victim better.

THE COMEDY/DRAMA REENACTMENT SHOW

There is another type of Reenactment Show that is much lighter than the Crime or Medical one. These may involve crimes or medical conditions, but their focus is more on the humor of the incident rather than the severity of it.

An example of a Comedy/Drama *Crime* Story might be about a burglar who tries to sneak into a house by coming down the chimney and gets stuck.

A Comedy/Drama *Medical* Story might be something like two people fighting to get the last pickle from a jar. They both reach in at the same time and both get their hands stuck in the jar.

With each of the above examples, something relatively serious has happened but the focus will be more on the humor rather than any serious consequences. The Actor auditioning for the Victim in these type of shows usually needs to play it deadly serious. They've got a problem that needs to be solved.

The other parts involved, be they Law Enforcement, Medical Personnel or Witnesses, can allow a little humor to enter their audition but only after they've determined that no serious harm has occurred or will occur to the Victim. Like the rule for Comedy vs. Drama, take the situation and lighten it up a bit and you'll find the humor.

CHAPTER 18

PHYSICALITY IN AUDITIONS

TO MOVE OR NOT TO MOVE

Actors and actresses are constantly asking me what to do in an audition when the scene calls for a physical action of some kind or another.

"It says I kiss her, what do I do?"

"I'm supposed to have a gun. Should I bring a prop to the audition?"

Let's break this down into three parts.

     1- Personal Physicality
     2- Inter-character Physicality
     3- Prop-related Physicality

PERSONAL PHYSICALITY'S

A Personal Physicality is an action a character performs alone without any type of prop. It can be something as simple as "Irene scratches her head," to quite involved, such as "Jack punches his head with his fists, stands up and runs about the room, screaming like a madman."

A good rule to follow when deciding what to do with any sort of physicality written in a scene is to ask: "Is it *necessary* to the personality of the character or the flow of the scene?"

Scratching your head or any other type of innocuous movement is most often not necessary. I say most often, because there are times when such a small, physical movement might be part of a character's psychological space. If a character is developing or has an ongoing physical tick, then I'd say it is part of this character. If the character is written as someone who scratches his head when he gets nervous, then the writer has included it for a specific reason, and not just to add a movement to indicate the state of being the writer envisions for this character at this time.

But even if it seems to be part of a specific direction with regards to the mental and physical state of this character, is it really *necessary*? If it is mentioned in the dialogue, either by your character or another character, then yes. If the scene says that Irene scratches her head then is followed by dialogue such as:

```
                    IRENE
          Damn it, I always
          scratch my head when
          I'm nervous.
```

Or

```
                    JOHN
          Irene, you're scratch-
          ing you head, I know
          you're lying.
```

In cases such as these I'd say, do the movement.

But if it is *not* necessary to the scene leave it out, unless you truly feel a *genuine* urge to do the movement. But it must be an integral part of who you are as this character, and it must grow out what is *happening to you at that moment*. Doing a movement just because it is written without any personal reason for doing it will appear forced and not natural. Your own way of expressing nervousness, whether it has physical movements or not, is going to be much stronger.

For example, the writers might include a physical movement because they want to make it clear what they feel a character's emotional state is at the time. They might write, "Bill paces the room," during a scene to indicate a high state of nerves or anxiety. But doing this during an audition will make it very difficult to film. Rather, understand the emotional state of the character and let that state be a part of your audition in a less physical way.

When deciding whether to do any physical movement in an audition, be aware that physical movements, in general, are distracting. When you make a move during an audition, everyone's eyes go to the movement. If it is not completely organic to you at that moment, it will read as false. Better to do nothing than make a false move. So if it is not necessary to advance the scene, leave a movement out.

WHEN TO MOVE

If the movement *is* necessary to the scene, if it takes the scene in another direction or, more importantly, if it takes the character in another direction *emotionally*, then do it. But be aware of size. If it is a large movement, you're much better off doing a *suggestion* of the movement. Big movements in auditions are *very* distracting and generally are to be avoided. There are times when a large physical movement is great, but rarely. Most auditions are filmed, with the shot being fairly close. Too big a movement will dominate the frame and appear HUGE to anyone watching it later. It also may be out of frame so the only thing the camera will capture will be a swash of unclear movement as the move crosses in front of the camera before going out of frame. If you do have a large movement that is an integral part of the story, as sometimes is the case in comedies and action stories, be sure and ask the frame of the camera. For example if you have to do a comedic bow, you don't want to bow out of frame. Whatever the comedic move make sure it is small enough so that the entire move, including your face, is always on camera. The same is true for an action story. If the script says you slug someone, a large and fast swing will only be a wave of out-of-focus movement if the frame is close on you. Better to do a small punch and tensing up of your muscles. That will give you the emotional connection to the movement, which is what they need to see in an audition.

ENHANCE BUT DON'T DISTRACT

If you do decide to include physical movement, make sure it doesn't backfire on you. I once watched an actor so involved in a scene that in his fervor he slammed his hand down upon the Casting Director's desk. Every eye in the room left his face and his performance and focused on the pens that flew out of a cup sitting a few inches away from where he slammed the desk. The movement was so big and so disruptive that it worked against him, no matter how much it might have affected him emotionally.

INTER-CHARACTER PHYSICALITY

Don't ever invade another person's space in an audition. EVER. If the scene calls for you to hit another character, there are a number of things you can do, depending on how it affects you. You can make a medium to small, quick gesture, such as slapping the air in front of you. You can hit your leg. You can hit a piece of furniture, but beware this could backfire on you like it did for the actor who knocked the pens all over the desk. But whatever movement you do, *keep it small*, no matter how much of it is described in the script. Get to the dialogue. If the movement happens at the end of the scene, again make it short and sweet. Better to focus on what that movement did to you. Did "hitting" the other character make you feel good or bad?

The same is true if you're the one at the end of a physical movement by another character. If you are hit in a scene, a *small* movement showing your body's reaction to the movement is fine. More important is what that action did to you emotionally. Did getting hit make you mad, afraid, hurt?

It's a good idea to keep any physical gesture or movement you make as close to your own body as you can. Not only will it be caught on camera, no one's eyes will wander far from your face, which is what they're mostly watching in an audition. This is an audition, so you are not expected to be in the scene physically as much as you are emotionally. Everyone knows once on set, with a fight choreographer and stunt coordinator, any physical confrontation will be safe and look convincing on film. In the audition, you only need to give a representation of physical confrontation, and one that doesn't make anyone in the room worry about safety.

The same rule applies to an affectionate gesture such as a caress. You can caress your script if it is an organic gesture that affects you. But the movement needs to do something to you and not be just a random touching.

WHEN BIG MOVES ARE NEEDED

Sometimes a big move is necessary in order for everyone to judge whether you are capable of a necessary action, such as a particular dance move or a gymnastic ability like a flip. In such cases the camera operator will open up the frame as wide as he can. But you still have to ask how much of the room you can use and still be in frame.

WARNING: If you *can repeatedly* do a required move not only well but under pressure, then go ahead. But DO NOT LIE AND SAY YOU CAN DO WHAT YOU REALLY CAN'T, even if you think you can learn and/or perfect the move by the time of the shoot. You'll only end up wasting everyone's time and embarrassing yourself; or worse, you'll get hurt.

DON'T KISS AND TELL

Kissing is a bit more problematic. Nothing is worse, or more laughable, than an actor or actress "making out" with the air. In an audition, it's not the kiss that is important, but how that kiss affects you. So instead of spending time worrying how or what you're going to kiss, examine the script to see what the effect of the kiss is and give that your focus and attention. If you absolutely need to, you can kiss your script or hand, but make it quick. The payoff of any intimate act is how it *affects* you, *not the act itself.*

That is a pretty good rule in general when dealing with any Inter-Character Physicality. Look at the scene and decide if the movement is really necessary. If it isn't just allow the *effect* of the movement to be present in your work and *skip* the movement.

PROP PHYSICALITY

Once again, is the character's involvement with a prop a necessary element in the growth of the scene? Sipping coffee, eating dinner or drinking a martini aren't necessary actions in an audition. They are things you are doing in the scene, and as such, what they tell you and the audience about your character's mental and emotional state is much more important than watching an actor pantomiming them. Focus on what is going on in the scene between the characters and let the knowledge of the physicality affect you without pretending to do it. Does sipping a martini make you feel sophisticated and in control or are you having a strong drink because you desperately need something to calm you down? In either case it's a much better choice to let the *reason* the drink is in the scene be part of *Who* and *How* you are. Unless the character is a performing mime, pretending you have a drink in your hand will only distract and not enhance.

Never bring in a prop for the audition. The minute you bring out a prop everyone's attention goes to the prop. Now it becomes an audition about a prop and not about you. I don't care what it is, even if it's a paper clip, my feeling is you don't need it.

BUT WHAT IF THE SCENE IS A PHONE CONVERSATION?

Many actors ask if they should use their cell phones if the scene is a phone conversation. This is the only time it might be ok to use a cell phone as a prop, but I would still say no. All you need to do is to direct your attention to the phone call. To do so *do not look directly at the reader*. It's a phone call so unless you're on a video call, you can't see the other person. Keep your face open to the reader and/or the camera, but allow yourself the luxury of being able to react physically without looking directly at anyone.

WEAPONS

A weapon is tricky. If you use the weapon against the other character in the scene, then a small movement is all that is needed, no matter how grand the movements are in the script. Bringing in an actual weapon prop, even if it is obviously a fake, is a big NO. Even a silly rubber knife takes a couple of seconds for everyone else in the room to realize it's not real. After that, their attention is on their relief that it's not real and their annoyance that you distracted them and made them worry about their safety, even if it was for only a couple of seconds.

Everyone watching your audition *knows* you have a gun in the scene. Rather than pointing your finger at the reader and pretending it's a gun, let the feeling of having a gun, of having someone else's life in your hands affect you. Be the person with a gun, and not merely an actor pretending to have one.

If you shoot the other character, you can make a small body movement if you want, but more importantly let the fact that you just shot somebody affect you. You don't need to say "BANG" (I've actually seen that happen!). Just be affected by the fact that you just shot or killed another person at that moment.

DIE GRACEFULLY

The same holds true if you're the one shot or stabbed. You don't need to create a whole death scene by flying backwards or bending over and falling on the floor. React physically to the assault, but make it as small as you can. If your character is not killed, then the *effect* of the assault is what is important. If your character is killed in the scene, a small slump is fine, whether you're sitting or standing. The scene, at least as far as your audition is concerned, is over the minute you're dead, so unless it is written as a grand, comedic death scene, chances are the Casting Director will cut the scene once you're shot or stabbed, if they even let it go that far.

CHAPTER 19

IN THE AUDITION ROOM

You have an audition! Terrific news. You've done your Prep work, but now what? You know what to do to prepare for the audition, but what do you do when it comes time to actually audition?

WHAT TO WEAR

Actors frequently stress out over the many things, and what to wear at an audition is high on this list. But it needn't be. If you follow some simple guidelines you need never spend more than a little time picking out what to wear.

What is the character wearing? If it is modern day dress and not something out of the ordinary, then wear something that is as close to that as your wardrobe allows. Do not worry about matching the wardrobe exactly. It's more important to wear something that has a similar *feel*. If the character is in a coat and tie, wear a coat and tie. If you don't have a coat and tie, wear something relatively conservative. The same if the character is in a ball gown. You don't have to dig out your prom dress, just wear something that gives a feeling of elegance, even it is only a simple dress. If the character is in a bathing suit, you don't have to come in a Speedo unless the Casting Director has specifically requested that. Just wear casual attire, maybe some shorts and a tee shirt. The point is to dress in the same tone as the character without your outfit being a distraction.

COSTUMES

If the character is in a costume of some kind, like a uniform, or is from a different time period, pick something of your own that has a similar tone. Think about the character's clothes and how those clothes affect him. A soldier wearing a dress uniform would feel quite differently than if he were in combat fatigues. A woman in an Elizabethan court dress would have a completely different demeanor than a girl in a miniskirt. If you pick something that suggests to you the manner, demeanor and tone of the character, it will work for everyone else in the room as well. Do not go in costume, even if it is something you already own. If you do most likely the costume will upstage you as everyone will be focusing on your outfit and not on your acting. You're not auditioning for the job of costumer, so let wardrobe do their work and you do yours.

WHAT DO I SAY WHEN I GO IN?

It's always nice to say hello to the Casting Director when entering the audition room, but don't go overboard. I generally don't shake anyone's hand unless they extend their hand first. This is not because of some sort of power play. The Casting Director is seeing many people in a day, many times a hundred or more. Shaking hands with everyone would not only take time, at the end of the day their hand would ache. So I let them decide whether a handshake is appropriate or not.

Greet the Casting Director but if there is room full of people do not go around greeting each one unless they are all introduced to you. A simple glance around the room, taking everyone and quietly acknowledging them is sufficient. If someone catches you eye and wants to ask you a question or two they will. You're there to show them your work not hold polite conversation. Give a great audition and there will be plenty of time for chitchat on the set.

Most importantly, be aware of the atmosphere of the room. Is everyone smiling at you and relaxed, or do they appear rushed? Does the Casting Director seem to be in a bit of a hurry with a waiting room full of actors, or is he more relaxed? You have to *read* the mood of the room. Some rooms are welcoming and others feel like you just walked into a military court martial.

It's easy to relax when everyone is warm and friendly, but what do you do when they're not? Don't worry about it. If everyone is tense when you walk in the room, it has nothing to do with you. In Television particularly, any number of things can cause tension in the people auditioning you. Deadlines altered at the last minute, production problems, casting problems, all can affect the tension level of the room. You didn't cause the tension, but you could improve the tension level by giving a *great* audition. If you're *confident* and *focused* you can ease the tension, maybe even erase it. If you do your job superbly, you may have just fixed one of their problems, casting a role.

The Casting Director will direct you as to how he would like the audition to proceed. He'll tell you who you're reading with and ask if you have any questions.

ASK ONLY WHAT YOU NEED TO KNOW

Hopefully most of the questions you have about the material have already been answered by your own research or by asking an assistant sitting in the outer office. If you were unable to get an answer about a story question or about a strange name pronunciation, then ask, but be brief. Asking lots of questions in the audition room puts everyone off. It says that you didn't take the time and effort to do your own research.

Do NOT ask how they would like to see you play the role. This is one of the worse questions you could ever ask. Show them your interpretation first. If they want it done differently, they will give you an adjustment. They want you to audition to see what you bring to the role. If they need to see something specific, they will tell you. I'll talk more about adjustments in a bit.

DO I SIT OR DO I STAND?

Most Casting Directors will let you make the decision to sit or stand, unless there is a compelling reason one way or the other, such as ease of filming the audition. What is the character doing in the scene? If the character is sitting, then sit. If he is standing or walking, then stand. But if you do stand, be sure not to wander about or lean from one side to the other. Stand in one place. If you're being filmed it's difficult for the camera operator to keep you in frame if you walk around. Even if you're not being filmed, it's easier for everyone to focus on your face if you don't move around.

You can also consider what the reader is doing. If the reader is sitting then if you sit you will be closer to eye level than if you stand. Conversely, if the reader is standing, you'll be looking up at them if you sit.

But above all, if you have a choice, do *whatever works best for you*. If you tend to be a bit hyper and move a lot, sitting might help focus you and reduce extraneous movement. If you tend to be more laid back with a lower energy, standing might give you a little extra nudge. But unless you're instructed to do one or the other make your own decision and make it confidently. If you choose to sit, take the chair firmly and position it properly with regard to the camera. If the chair is already in place, sit down as if you a CEO meeting with his board of directors. If you choose to stand, firmly take a stance don't wander aimlessly into place. It's your audition and the sooner you take charge and present yourself as a pro who is there to work the sooner you'll grab their attention and hold it.

WHERE IS THE CAMERA?

Practically all Film and Television auditions are videoed. Whether you sit or stand, be aware of the camera's position. Is it to one side or directly in front of you? Where is the reader sitting in relation to the camera? You want to make sure *as much of your face is on camera as possible*, so you might have to "cheat," or tilt your head to one side or the other slightly to make that happen. The more of your face that is recorded the better anyone watching later can judge your audition. It is most likely that the people with the power to hire you will only be seeing the filmed version of your audition. No matter who is in the room during the filming, if as much of your face as possible isn't on camera you're not showing the decision makers as much of you as you can.

SLATING

You may be asked to *Slate* before you begin reading the sides. Slating is simply looking directly into the camera and stating your name. Sometimes the Casting Director will ask you to state more information, such as the role you're reading for and/or your agent. Other times after you state the initial information they will ask you a couple of questions, such as how tall you are or whether you have a specific skill needed for the character. Answer any and all questions as simply as possible. This doesn't mean you have to answer like a robot, without any personality. It means don't add extra time by giving them a four sentence reply to a yes or no question.

Do I slate in character? Depends. Generally I think it's best not to slate in character. Everybody knows you're an actor and not the actual character you're reading for. However I would suggest slating in a demeanor appropriate to the project and character you're reading for. If it is a light comedy, your slate should be pleasant, light and with an honest smile. If it is an intense drama, you don't need to slate like a serial killer in a mug shot, but your slate should be a simple, direct addressing to the camera.

ACCENTS

If your character has an accent, and you're using the accent in your audition, I would suggest slating in that accent. But before you use an accent, *make sure you do it very well*. Not only do you have to do it well, you have to be understood. You may have a natural or be able to do a spot-on Cockney accent, but if it is so authentic that nobody outside the center of London can understand you, it will cost you the job.

WHAT DO I DO WITH THE SIDES?

Always hold your sides in your hand, even if you have them completely memorized. This is an audition, not a final performance. You're showing everyone what you can do at this point, at the beginning of your being involved with the project. If you put the pages down, you're saying that what you're showing them is your final and fixed performance.

Another reason to hold the sides is that even though you had them completely memorized, for some reason during the audition you might forget a line or be thrown off by something. If you have the sides in your hand, you only have to glance down to find your place. I've had several Casting Directors tell me they get nervous when an actor puts his sides down and are distracted throughout the audition because they're constantly wondering when and if he'll forget a line. By holding the sides you take away a reason for them not to be completely focused on you and your audition.

WHAT DO I DO IF I MAKE A MISTAKE DURING THE READING?

Unless the mistake is at the very beginning, or something major like skipping a large section of the material, *keep going*. The mistake will be forgotten seconds later if you keep going. If you stop or apologize, or in any way acknowledge the mistake, you're only accenting it and drawing attention to it. We all make mistakes in everyday life. We mispronounce words and fumble over them all the time. If you're involved in the life situation of the scene, the interaction between the characters is what is important, not whether you flubbed a word or two. If you stop to apologize or make fun of your mistake, you take yourself and everyone watching out of the scene. Now they see an actor who made a mistake and not a character who happened to flub some words.

If you've made a mistake at the very beginning that has gotten you off track, you can ask to start again. The Casting Director may very well ask you to start again if he feels you'd be better off starting off fresh. Don't belabor the point, apologizing and making a big deal over what went wrong, simply start again and get right into it. If you've made a major mistake well into the reading, I would not suggest stopping and asking to start again unless it is absolutely necessary. If you've left out a page or some vital information and there is no way to pick it up without stopping, then fine. But only ask to start again when *there is no way you can continue*. You may have been terrific despite the mistake, and if you start again you might become self-conscious and so intent on not making the same mistake that your reading will suffer.

But if you desperately feel you need to start over, or if the Casting Director asks you start again, take a breath and a moment to focus. Before you do start again, be sure you understand what went wrong and know how to avoid making the same mistake again.

WHAT DO I DO AFTER I'VE FINISHED READING?

The reading is not over until the Casting Director says it is. It doesn't make any difference who has the last line, *stay in the scene until the Casting Director ends it*. Many times the last line of a scene introduces a major point. Whether this line is yours or not, give yourself the luxury of experiencing how this point affects you. You don't have to have a line to have a reaction to what you've been told. If you stay in the scene you'll keep their interest, especially since the camera is on your face.

If they have seen what they needed to see they will thank you. If they need to see more they will ask for an *adjustment*. If they do not ask for an adjustment thank them for seeing you, get up and walk out. DO NOT ASK IF THEY WANT TO SEE IT A DIFFERENT WAY. No matter how you think you did, if they want to see something different they will ask. *Under no circumstances apologize for anything*. If you forgot a line, or didn't do something in the scene you so badly wanted to, let it go. They may have loved what you did. If you go into an explanation of why you feel it wasn't your best work, you've done nothing but add doubt and negativity to their opinion of your audition.

ADJUSTMENTS

Many actors are terrified of the dreaded *adjustment*. "They hated me!" Banish that thought right now. Adjustments are *good things*. It means the Casting Director sees something in you he likes and wants to work with you, to direct you and give you a change of focus. The Casting Director has been working on the project much longer than you have. He has information you don't, such as how the Director or Producer may want a scene to go. Listen to the adjustment. Is it something major, such as a change in the whole demeanor of the character, or is it a specific adjustment in a certain section of the side? Whatever it is, make sure you understand precisely what you're being asked to do. If you don't, ASK. Better to take a couple of extra seconds getting clarification then not give him what he asked for. But be brief. When a Casting Director asks for an adjustment he is not asking for a ten minute discussion on the themes and deep interior motives of the character. He is giving you a direction and he expects you to understand it and implement it. If you're unclear, be specific about what it is you're unclear about.

Once you understand the adjustment, MOVE. If you're standing, take a few steps. If you're sitting, get up if you can, or at the very least change your position. It has been proven time and time again that physical movement helps creativity. By moving your body, even slightly, you're freeing yourself to add the adjustment.

DON'T THROW EVERYTHING YOU DID OUT

Most often an adjustment is not a total redo but a change in focus in one or two places. That means they liked much if not most of what you did. They don't want you to get rid of what they did like, only to add or "adjust" certain things. So do what you did before, but stay open to not only adding the adjustment but to allowing the adjustment and the subsequent reaction to the adjustment by the reader to affect you.

If the adjustment is a total redo, then so be it. Take the adjustment and let it redirect you. This is exactly why you worked with *opposite choices* in your prep work. You've already looked at the scene from many different angles, so chances are any adjustment you're given, no matter how extreme, isn't that far from what you've already played with. That was one of the reasons for working with *opposite choices*, to enable you to be flexible. Embrace that flexibility and see where it takes you and the scene. Even if it isn't exactly what the Casting Director envisioned, by freely going with the adjustment you're showing them you are open to direction.

THE AUDITION IS OVER, NOW WHAT?

Congratulate yourself on a great audition and go on with your life. Try not to replay the audition over and over in your head or go through the scene in your car on the way home. It is helpful to objectively look at what you did to see where you were great and where you might have not been so great. But look at it *objectively*. Did you not take an adjustment as far as you should? Did you find your nerves getting in the way? Did you forget the camera location and turn away from it too much? Whatever you objectively feel you could improve, be specific. Making a general statement such as "I sucked!" is pointless and counterproductive.

KEEP AN AUDITION DIARY

I would strongly suggest keeping an audition diary. In addition to recording who you saw, what the project was, who was in the room, etc., write down your own feelings as to how the audition went from your perspective. Did any mistakes happen that you can prevent in the future? What types of mistakes were they, *technical* or *creative*? By technical I mean something like not being able to find your place in the side easily or dropping a page because it wasn't stapled. Was the print big enough on the side or should you enlarge it for your next audition? Whatever technical problems you might have had, there is a solution. Think about the problem and the solution will most probably readily appear. If not, bring it up with your audition coach or other actors to see how they handle the same problem.

Were the mistakes creative? Did you freeze up and find yourself unable to genuinely react to what was happening in the reading or find yourself pulling back from a choice because you felt unsure? Whatever happened, make a note of it and make a plan to deal with it. Bring it up with your teacher or coach or find some other way to specifically address it. Make a plan to fix it, and then let it go.

AN AUDITION IS NOT THE BEGINNING OR END OF YOUR LIFE

Auditions are important and giving a great audition is extremely important, but auditions are not the end-all and be-all of your life. *They are but steps in the process of building a career.* Sure, you want as many of your auditions to be as great as possible, but even great auditions don't *guarantee* you'll be hired. What they most often do guarantee is that you'll be remembered and brought back. But just as a great audition doesn't guarantee you'll be hired a not-so-great one doesn't mean you should give up acting. Instead of wallowing in self-pity after a not-so-great audition, let it be a learning experience. Note the things that need work and make a plan on how to fix them; then move on.

After an audition, do something you enjoy. Get some ice cream, go for a bike ride, whatever it is that feels like a reward, do it. You just put yourself out there in front of other people, and put your work, talent and inner being on the line. Look at each audition as a mini-performance, a chance to create and live inside a character's life instead of a job interview. The fact that it *is* a job interview doesn't mean that your unique artistic expression is any less real; it just means that the audience is going to choose how they react to that expression. They may give you a job or they may not, they may call you in for something else right away or it may be months before you're back in that office. But whatever the case, it doesn't take away from or add to what you did, to the life you created in the audition.

You should reward yourself for that creation. With each audition you're adding to your hire-ability, because after each audition you're that much more experienced. With each great audition you're also adding to the opinion the Casting Director has about you and your work. With each great audition you have the opportunity to open the door to another audition. Keep opening doors long enough and you'll be asked to stick around.

CHAPTER 20

TELEVISION AND FILM AUDITION DO'S AND NEVER DO'S

Both from my own experience as an actor and coach, as well as talking to Casting Directors, I've compiled my list Things To Do and Never Do at an Audition. Many of them may sound absurdly obvious, but often when we're under stress we make absurdly simple mistakes. I'll never forget one particularly embarrassing incident that happened to me early in my career. I was fairly young and had been booking one job right after another. I was "hot," at least in my own mind. I went in to read for a Series Regular in a pilot. There were several people in the room. Though I knew no one besides the Casting Director and the others were not introduced to me, I assumed they were the heads of the production team. I read the scene, they thanked me and I left the room. In the waiting room I saw a good friend of mine. He was sitting near the front desk where a young intern was on the phone. My friend asked how I did and I replied, "Great, I think. There's only so much you can do with shit writing." My friend and I laughed and I left. Later that day my agent called me. He told that I didn't get the role because the "writer didn't want me to have to stoop to doing shit writing." The man on the phone in the lobby who I thought was a lowly intern was the creator and head writer of the pilot. Oops.

THINGS TO DO

1 – **Be prepared**. You will almost always get sides in advance of your audition. Make sure you take the time you need to prepare. If you are given new sides when you arrive at an audition, or are getting them for the first time, go somewhere quiet and prepare for ten to fifteen minutes. Just make sure you do not sign in until you're ready, even if there is a long list of people who have signed in before you. Once you've signed in you've signaled that you're present and ready to go.

2 – **Show up on time**. If you can't make your scheduled time slot, make arrangements for a different time as far ahead of time as possible. Nothing shows unprofessionalism like waltzing into an audition late, no matter what the reason.

3 – **Know how to pronounce names and terms**. If you don't know how to pronounce something, do your research beforehand or ask an associate in the office *before* you go into the audition.

4 – **Know the Casting Director's name**. You'd be surprised how many actors don't pay attention to the Casting Director's name.

5 – **Handle your sides effortlessly**. It is very distracting when an actor makes huge movements and noises when turning the pages of a side. If you have a multi-page side, see if there is some way you can cut and paste it into fewer pages.

6 – **Take Ownership of your Work and Choices**. You've prepared yourself; now do what you've prepared *confidently*.

7 – **Listen carefully to all adjustments**. Don't just nod you head and say "ok," make sure you fully understand the adjustment.

8 – **Move before adjusting**. Take a couple of seconds to ingest the adjustment while moving your body, either by taking a few steps or repositioning yourself in your chair.

9 – **Listen carefully to any pre-audition information or adjustments**. Often the Casting Director will give you last-minute information either personally or to the entire waiting room. This might be because a number of actors reading before you made the same mistake due to a misunderstanding of the side, or because a story point has changed. Listen to this as you would an adjustment and make changes accordingly so that when you go into the room you've already incorporated that adjustment into your audition.

10 – **Be aware of the camera**. Know where it is and how it is filming you. Ask the frame so you know how much of you it is getting and how much freedom of movement you have before you're out of frame.

11 – **Leave when it's over**. Don't try to prolong your time in front of them by telling a wild story or rambling on how much you love the show. They're busy and they'll respect you a lot more if you respect their time. No one gets hired because *they love* a show; they get hired because they give an audition the *show will love*.

12 – **Treat** *everyone* **in the office with respect**. That person you give a hard time to today because they don't have the bathroom key may very well be the Casting Director of a project tomorrow. Treat everyone at the casting office with respect and kindness regardless of what you think their position is.

13 – Wear clothing that is character appropriate. I'm not saying put together an exact ensemble as described in the sides, but if the character is a businessman don't come in shorts and a tank top. Dressing in a manner that suggests the character will not only help them see you as right *for* the part, it will make you feel right *in* the part.

THINGS TO NEVER DO

1 – **Never make excuses**. You're representing yourself as a professional. If you just got the sides, it is probably because they weren't available earlier. Everyone reading for the same role is in the same situation. Don't make excuses for how bad you think you're reading is going to be, just do your best work. If the sides were available ahead of time but for some reason you didn't look at them until just before your audition, just go in and do your very best work. If you don't feel you can do your best work, cancel the audition. If you go in with an excuse, you're giving them an excuse not to hire you.

2 – **Never blame traffic for being late**. There's traffic everywhere, especially in major cities, and everybody has to deal with it. Allow plenty of time to arrive at your audition on time.

3- **Never shake the Casting Director's hand unless it's offered**. The same goes for anyone else in the room. I'm not advising you to be rude or distant, but practical. They're seeing a large number of actors, possibly over several days. Shaking that many hands can be painful, not to mention unsanitary. Let them make the choice to shake or not.

4- **Never go into a long monologue when asked if you have any questions**. If you truly have a question that you need answered before you read, then ask it briefly and succinctly. Don't make it a lengthy discussion about the script.

5 – **Never ask how they want you to do it**. Do what you've prepared and show them *your take* on the scene. If they want you to do it differently they'll give you an adjustment. Better to show them your own creativity first, otherwise they'll only see the scene from their specific direction. Even if your initial take was the same as theirs, they won't attribute it to your understanding of the script as much as they will their direction.

6 – **Never tell them how you're going to do a scene**. Just do it. If you tell them what you plan to do ahead of time and you don't do it exactly as you said, they'll think you can't even do what you planned. If you do it as you said then the surprise is gone and the read won't be as exciting to watch.

7 – **Never argue with a Casting Director.** Just because you think the adjustment you've been given is wrong, it doesn't matter. They know the script and what the Producer and Director want. Just take the adjustment and do your best. Your first read may very well have been perfect and they merely want to see how well you can take direction.

8- **Never bring props to an audition, especially a weapon of any kind, even if fake**. All props do is take focus away from you. Using a cell phone if the scene is about a phone call is about the only exception, but even then it isn't necessary and can actually hamper your audition as you will have only one hand to easily turn the pages of your sides. They know the scene, they know on set you'll have all the props you will need. They want to see your initial take of the human side of the scene, not how well you handle props.

9 – **Never wear a costume to an audition**. Even if you have the actual costume, such as a soldier's uniform or a police uniform or waitresses outfit. Coming in costume is like a gimmick. It draws attention to itself and thereby takes attention away from what you are bringing of yourself to the audition. The only exception is if the Casting Director has expressly requested a costume to be worn. And even then, make sure it isn't so elaborate it upstages you.

10 – **Never touch the Casting Director or Reader**. No matter what it says you do in the scene, don't try to kiss them, don't push them, don't shake their hand. Not only does it violate their personal space, if the audition is being filmed it will most likely take you out of frame. You can make a gesture that is indicative of the move or of how the move affects you if necessary.

11 – **Never make derogatory comments about the script or the show.** No one cares if you think the script is badly written. Your job is to do your best with whatever material you're given. Show them you're a team player by really trying to make it work. If you truly think the script is garbage and would be embarrassed having anything to do with it then don't accept the audition.

12 – **Never ask if there are going to be callbacks.** With most auditions being filmed these days, callbacks are rare. Anyone who needs to see your audition who wasn't in the room the first time will be able to see the filmed version. In the rare instances where there are callbacks, if the Casting Director needs to call you back they will tell you any information you need to know about

callbacks. Asking about callbacks is like asking how you did. It puts them in an awkward position. If you're leaving town in a matter of hours and plan to be away for a couple of days, you can mention that. Do so only to let them know that while you can be contacted either personally or via your agent, physically you'll be unavailable for a brief time period should they want to see you again.

13 - **Never forget to enjoy yourself**. You have an audition! How great is that? Have fun and use this wonderful opportunity to create a character's life, even if you only have one word. Your sense of enjoyment and commitment will shine through and many times those attributes will get you hired, especially in auditions where there is not much dialogue.

CHAPTER 21

EPILOGUE

The Secret weapon

I've saved the best for last. The nuclear option, the one thing that will blow everyone else out of the water.

Now that you've read the sides, you've dissected them, made choices appropriate for the side and the medium, done all your research, watched an episode or two of the Television show, familiarized yourself with the film's producer's and writer's other credits, you've got one last weapon in your arsenal.

YOU.

"What," you ask me, "are you crazy? I'm no secret weapon, I'm just 'little ol' me.'" Yes, you are just little ol' you. But though there are billions of people in the world, there is only one you. The way you view and react to the world is unique to you, and no one, anywhere, does it exactly like you do.

You, with all your attributes and flaws, are absolutely perfect for the part. All you have to do is let that *you* shine through, unmonitored and unrestrained.

How do you do that? Simple. Forget every bit of work you've done on the side. Throw it away.

"What?" you ask. "After all the time and energy I just spent doing everything you told me to do, you want me to throw it away?" Yep, that's exactly what I'm asking you to do.

If you've done your work carefully, you've already begun to throw it away. When you dissected the sides, you were using your conscious mind. You read through the sides making note of the content, style and tone of the material. You noted every direction and change of direction. But as you went back over the sides and began to make choices, your subconscious mind began to awaken. Some choices were obvious while others seemed to come from nowhere. They didn't come from nowhere, they came from you. Some instinct, some gut feeling led you to those choices, especially the ones you come upon after you explored the side using your *opposite* choices. In those times your conscious mind stood back and your subconscious mind and talent stepped forward. Now it is time to let them both step forward even more.

To let that happen you have to let go of the idea that you need to cling to the decisions you made and constantly remind yourself about them. You made them; they are already a part of you and your interpretation of the sides. It's like riding a bicycle, once you've learned how you don't need to constantly remind yourself to balance and steer. Your mind and body do it naturally, subconsciously. The same is true during an audition. You've done your work, you know WHO you are, WHERE you are, WHEN you are, WHAT you're doing, WHY you're doing it and have made choices as to HOW this side initially affects you. Now it's time to throw *yourself* into the audition experience.

Any side is a story, and that story represents life from a unique perspective. In life, no matter how thoroughly we prepare for anything, work, play, love, it most often *never goes quite how we planned*. Sometimes things veer slightly from what we expected, other times everything soars off in a completely unexpected direction. That's life. That's what makes it interesting and many times exciting.

An audition is also life. Yes, it's a story, but that doesn't make it any less than life. It is a story with real, living people sharing a life experience. And when you're in the audition room the story is *your life*. And just as in real life, people and things never are exactly as we expect them to be. No matter what we think or expect, in any life experience, anything can happen.

Trust yourself to *be* yourself and go with the flow. What does that mean, you might ask? It means no matter how many times you read the scene, no matter what the reader does or doesn't do, each time will be a unique experience. Allow yourself the freedom to respond to however the experience affects you.

If you got mad in a certain spot when you read the side before but this time you find it funny, go with it. If you felt sympathetic in one read but in the next you feel baffled, let it come through.

Honestly talk and respond to the reader. You already know all the circumstances of the side, don't think about them. They are a part of you, and if you put your focus on the reader and really take in everything about him as he responds to you, your audition will be instinctual and you will be *alive* in the room. Your responses will be colored by all the work you've done, but they will be unique and fresh because they will be born of whatever is happening to you each second. Even if the reader gives you exactly what you expected, it will never be *exactly* what you expected. He is a human being with his own feelings and nuances, and there will always be something just a bit different about what he gives you.

By being right there with the reader, by being attuned to everything he's giving you, obvious and subtle, you'll unleash your secret weapon. You'll create a spark by being willing to stand on the edge of the audition-cliff and jump in whatever direction you're inspired to do *each moment* of the audition. If you do that, you will *stop trying to be what they want*. Instead…

You will make them want what you are.

CHAPTER 22

RECOMMENDED READING

SCREENPLAY - The Foundations of Screenwriting
By Syd Field
Published by Dell Publishing 1984
ISBN: 0-440-57647-4

An excellent overview of how a traditional screenplay is structured.

SAVE THE CAT! The Last Book on Screenwriting You'll Ever Need
By Blake Snyder
Published by Michael Wiese Productions 2005
ISBN: 1-932907-00-9

THE WRITER'S JOURNEY – Mythic Structure For Storytellers and Screenwriters
By Christopher Vogler
Published by Michael Wiese Productions 1992
ISBN: 0-941188-13-2
A great resource on how timeless myths and archetypes are used in storytelling.

ABOUT THE AUTHOR

Kevin Scott Allen has been a professional film and television actor for over thirty years. His extensive credits include feature films as well as television shows ranging from Episodic Dramas to Sit-Coms. In addition to acting, he is a well known and sought out on-camera acting teacher and audition coach in Los Angeles, California. His students' successful auditions have won them starring roles in films as well as co-star, guest star and series regular roles in television. Web site: www.kevinscottallen.com

More books from Kevin+Scott+Allen are available at:
http://ReAnimus.com/store/?author=Kevin+Scott+Allen

ReAnimus Press

Breathing Life into Great Books

If you enjoyed this book we hope you'll tell others or write a review! We also invite you to subscribe to our newsletter to learn about our new releases and join our affiliate program (where you earn 12% of sales you recommend) at
www.ReAnimus.com.

Here are more ebooks you'll enjoy from ReAnimus Press, available from ReAnimus Press's web site, Amazon.com, bn.com, etc.:

The Box: An Oral History of Television, 1920-1961, by
Jeff Kisseloff

You Must Remember This: An Oral History of Manhattan from the 1890s to World War II, by Jeff Kisseloff

Dear America: Letters Home from Vietnam, by edited
by Bernard Edelman for The New York Vietnam Veterans
Memorial Commission

I've Never Been To Me, by Charlene Oliver

The Resurrection of Frank Borchard, by Jerry Sohl

Prelude to Peril, by Jerry Sohl

The Lemon Eaters, by Jerry Sohl

Night Slaves, by Jerry Sohl

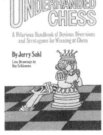

Underhanded Chess, by Jerry Sohl

Underhanded Bridge, by Jerry Sohl

Side Effects, by Harvey Jacobs

American Goliath, by Harvey Jacobs

Steep Deep & Dyslexic, by Jeffrey Bergeron

Darker Passions, by Edward Bryant

Passing Through the Flame, by Norman Spinrad

Little Heroes, by Norman Spinrad

In Search of the Big Bang, by John Gribbin

Cosmic Coincidences, by John Gribbin and Martin Rees

Q is for Quantum, by John Gribbin

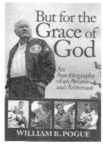

But for the Grace of God, by William R. Pogue

The Futurians, by Damon Knight

By The Sea, by Henry Gee

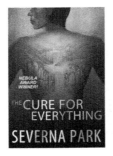

The Cure for Everything, by Severna Park

The Sweet Taste of Regret, by Karen Haber

Pictures at 11, by Norman Spinrad

The Altered Ego, by Jerry Sohl

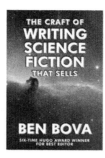

The Craft of Writing Science Fiction that Sells, by Ben Bova

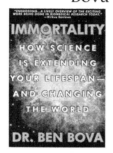

Immortality, by Ben Bova

The Multiple Man, by Ben Bova

Having Relationships With Characters on the Road to Great Fiction, by Andrew Burt

The Exiles Trilogy, by Ben Bova

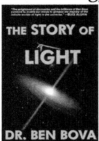

The Story of Light, by Ben Bova

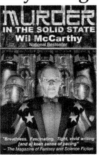

Murder in the Solid State, by Wil McCarthy

Innocents Abroad (Fully Illustrated & Enhanced Collectors' Edition), by Mark Twain

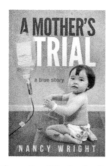

A Mother's Trial, by Nancy Wright

Bad Karma: A True Story of Obsession and Murder,
by Deborah Blum

Local Knowledge (A Kieran Lenahan Mystery), by
Conor Daly

Printed in Great Britain
by Amazon

15094590R00161